MORALITY
FOR
MODERNS

Marc Oraison

MORALITY FOR MODERNS

Postface by R. Simon

Translated by J. F. Bernard

Doubleday & Company, Inc., Garden City, New York
1972

This book was originally published in French as *Pour une Education Morale Dynamique* by Fayard-Mame, Paris, in the *Langages de la Foi* series. © I.S.P.C., 1971

Library of Congress Catalog Card Number: 70–181480

CONTENTS

Preface   9
1. Youth—A Symbol of Search   13
2. Morality—An Uncertain Science   31
3. False Values   41
4. The Ultimate Value: Love   65
5. Sexual Perspectives   73
6. A Dramatic Morality   89
Conclusion   105
Postface by R. Simon   107
Appendix   115

MORALITY
FOR
MODERNS

PREFACE

It's very difficult nowadays for someone of my age to speak to young people about "morals" and "morality." There is a very good chance that anyone who tries to do so will simply be ignored. Even the words *morals* and *morality* are suspect, because they seem to express the will of other people—that is, the will of adults; and this will is regarded as circumscribing, limiting, and forbidding, as preventing somehow the search for self-fulfillment and self-identity. Young people, when we speak to them of morals, seem to experience a reaction that is, at least superficially, paradoxical. They feel that our "morals" are designed to keep them from becoming the moral beings that they want to be. In other words, morality today carries with it the risk of leading eventually to "immoralism"—a situation that, in the final analysis, is probably the ultimate protest against everything that the word itself implies.

It must be admitted that the adult world is, in large part, responsible for this situation, albeit in good faith. When youth revolts—as they did, for example, in Paris in May and

June 1968—it may be that they have good reasons for revolting. This, however, is not to say that young people *ipso
facto* are "rejecting all morality." On the contrary, it seems
that they are entering upon a passionate search for moral
values that answer to their needs. One would have to be
blind not to see that at the heart of such uprisings there is
an immense treasure of human generosity; not a new
treasure, but one that conditions every historical movement, no matter how ambivalent it may be.

This generosity has a meaning. It is irrepressible, despite
the burden of illusions and conformities that may hinder
it. Man, through an uninterrupted chain of crises and upheavals, always seeks an ideal standard of behavior. We
live in a time of crisis and upheaval—a fact that is so universally acknowledged that the words are almost a cliché.
Now, is it possible for us, both adults and young people, together, united by a sense of human solidarity, to try to
determine the significance of that situation? We, the adults,
must listen to what our juniors are saying, and discern
what there is of value in it. And youth must realize that we
adults do not pretend to have all the answers; that we, too,
acknowledge the uncertainty of human destiny and know
that if we depend only upon ourselves, we will never be
able to solve our problems.

Thirty years from now, we middle-aged adults will
probably be dead, and the people who are young today will
have to live in the world we leave them. They, in their turn,
will have to deal with the restlessness of their own young
people. We have an obligation to prepare them in advance
not only to work out their own lives, but also to deal with
the inevitable confrontation between themselves and their

own children—a confrontation that will be at once their agony and their joy.

Such is the subject of this book.

A man who is fifty years old possesses only one thing of value: experience. Whatever he knows, therefore, is relative, since it is conditioned by that experience. And that is the problem when dealing with young people. A man *needs* to have certitude in knowing what he should do; and, because he is young, he does not yet have that certain knowledge from within himself. Of course, he is trying to learn, to discover a standard of behavior; and the first thing he does is learn what he should *not* do, because the only frame of reference he has is the behavior of adults. In other words, his first reaction is *against*. The important thing, in the long run, will be for him to reach the point where he can learn to be not *against*, and not necessarily *like*, but *with*.

After all, the aim of education, of human effort, of every reflection on the human condition, is simply this: to make every human being autonomous, and yet to enable him to "relate" to the rest of mankind.

This having been said, let us admit that this aim is virtually impossible to execute. Does this mean that we should abandon it? That is what we shall see.

Easter 1970.

1. YOUTH—
A SYMBOL OF SEARCH

Mobilis in mobile . . .

Captain Nemo's motto is a fair characterization of the general situation of youth in the contemporary world. It means "Movement in movement."

Youth, in effect, is, by definition, the human consciousness in search of itself—a search that has not yet reached a wholly satisfactory conclusion. Youth, in other words, is movement. And the contemporary world is also moving, changing, in such an obvious manner that it is superfluous to say so.

This movement, this change, has a very deep meaning of its own, a significance that, in the final analysis, may prove to be indecipherable. Yet, before contemplating such riddles of human behavior as lead inexorably to questions without answers—to "mysteries" in the proper sense of the word, we must define what we mean by "youth" and "young."

The adjective "young" designates a certain frame of mind: a flexibility, a readiness to adapt oneself to circum-

stances and to understand what was not previously understood. In this sense, youth is not necessarily synonymous
with tender years. There are people of twenty who were
never young, and people of eighty who have always been
young.

The noun "youth," on the other hand, designates a certain chronological span, a slice of one's existence as a
human being. We speak of childhood, youth, adulthood,
middle age, old age, and so forth. All of these are vague
terms, of course; but, generally speaking, we can say that
"youth" designates the period between the beginning of
adolescence and the time when a person has found his
place within the framework of complex social reality in the
broadest meaning of that term. It is obvious that the
chronological limits of youth are variable and depend upon
such things as social and cultural environment and educational opportunities. This particular aspect of the question
is a further complication, since—as a paradoxical conse-
quence of progress in science and technology—it often happens that a man or woman reaches adulthood at an age
that does not correspond to the end of his or her physical
development.

Since the period of youth is not uniform, we cannot really
distinguish its various stages very clearly without resorting
to generalities and artificial distinctions. A personality does
not develop suddenly, nor does it develop in a regular
manner through separate stages. The only stage that we
can really distinguish with any degree of certitude is the
beginning of development, which consists in the complex
phenomenon of psychosomatic puberty. According to contemporary anthropological data, a child's behavior, until

the time of puberty, is governed by his needs. A child's training, the structure of the superego, and the beginnings of moral awareness are all essentially imposed by the will, or the words, of other people. During the formative period, therefore, a child is given a system for living, a network of relations within which he is able (or unable) to find a place for himself, to be happy, and within which he develops according to his intellectual abilities and his need to learn. This is not at all to say that a child feels no need to assert himself or to act on his own. Even in the very early years, the yearning for autonomy and desire to act on one's own initiative is present, and a child often attempts to assert his own will in opposition to that of his parents. On the whole, however, what we can call a child's self-realization is assured by a human reality that is stronger than his own will, and that, in one way or another, has the final word. It is because of a child's acceptance of this state of dependency that, in spite of conflicts and problems, he finds the emotional climate necessary both to his continued existence and to his development.

The advent of puberty, for all practical purposes, means the beginning of a child's struggle for self-assertion and autonomy. At this point, it seems that the child suddenly becomes aware that the relationships in which he has hitherto existed are incapable of leading him to self-realization. The symptomatology of this stage in life is too well known to require reiteration. All we need do is bear in mind the single characteristic that holds true of human existence as a whole, but which is manifested in a particularly dramatic way at the stage of which we are speaking. That is, the adolescent is torn between two contradictory emo-

tional forces. One force pulls him toward the adventure of
a search for self; the other draws him back by means of a
sort of anguished nostalgia for the past. The adolescent
quickly realizes, more or less clearly, that henceforth he will
be responsible for his own behavior in every aspect of his
life—not himself alone (i.e., independently of everyone
else), but by himself and on his own initiative. In other
words, the adolescent, by virtue of an inexorable law of existence, now begins to accept responsibility for himself, to
become an adult in his own right in the eyes of the rest of
the world. His most important task at this time is to find a

point of reference in the positive and satisfying, although
conflict-ridden, search for himself. It goes without saying
that his search will be a constant battle between what the
outside world wants and what his own ideals propose. During this period, it is the outlook, or the consciousness, of
the adolescent that is in the process of full change. It is not
a comfortable process, and the adolescent suffers from it. It
is therefore inevitable that those around him feel the consequences of this suffering, since they, too, had, until now,
existed within an apparently well established network of relationships with the adolescent.

So, we may state that youth begins with the beginning of
this crisis of personal growth and development. But when
does it end? It is hard to say. All we can do is give general
and conventional answers; that is, we can only give a few
guidelines which, given the complexities of human life, are
quite variable. These guidelines may be formulated either
upon the basis of professional observation, or upon that of
an explicit recognition, within a social context, of the
sexual maturity of a subject. This constitutes an aspect

of marriage that is seldom emphasized. Paradoxically, we might say that when a couple embark on life together, their marriage is an assertion that they are fully integrated into the human society in which they will live in the fullness of their sexual commitment, even before it is an exclusive contract or a social convention.

It is obvious that, during this long period of interior unrest that we call youth, every young man and woman examines his whole life-style, his customary deportment, the direction of his energies—in other words, everything that constitutes his or her "moral life" in the proper meaning of that term. What the young person is doing, in fact, during this entire period of change, is attempting to find what, generally speaking, we may designate as his proper place in society. He is concerned about being able to live; and he is also concerned about being able to interpret life as being worth living. That is, he is trying—in one way or another, for better or worse—to find his own place in the midst of other people, and to work out his relationships with other people, from the two very different standpoints of his own previous relations and of what society expects of him.

During childhood, and under the inescapable influence of his educational environment, every subject more or less makes such an adjustment. With the onset of adolescence, however, when the subject stands at the threshold of a vast new world of human beings, he must depend upon his own resources in order to look for, and to achieve, that adjustment by virtue of which he will find sufficient happiness and security in life. It goes without saying that this search is not carried out in a vacuum. It is influenced and modified by other people, and not by those who are closest to the young man. The search for adjustment is, of necessity, modified by the life-style or the milieu in which the searcher lives; which is to say that it is inexorably affected by the kind of civilization or culture in which the subject will have to spend his life.

The act of searching in itself tends to lead to a certain stability, or at least to a minimal kind of permanence. And, at this point, we should stop and reflect upon a somewhat complex and contradictory concept: that of "duration." All of us, in fact, have the deep feeling that we are passing our lives in a time continuum that is special to ourselves, even though it is contemporaneous with the lives of others. At the same time, we all feel, even more deeply, the radical need to immobilize time, or at least to make it somehow supratemporal by eliminating change as much as possible. In other words, we are all fighting—even though it may not be a conscious fight—against an awareness that exists in all of us that our personal measure of time, which is the dynamic of our existence, leads to that essentially mysterious event which we call death. By means of a sort of tacit and universal agreement, mankind always tends to establish a way of living (a culture, or civilization, or life-style) that is regarded as being virtually definitive and immutable. Every structure of life in common, whatever its purpose or reason, tends to perpetuate itself as such, as though mankind wished, in spite of itself, to ignore that motion forward that is proper to man and is both man's treasure and the reminder of his own fragility.

In the moral search of the adolescent or of the young person, it is clear that the complex system of human conventions of the society in which he is attempting to find a place will play a very important part. The conflict—and it is a constructive conflict—occurs of necessity when the young person pits his own deep, personal aspirations, however nebulous they may be, against what society offers as its "values." To put it simply, the civilization in which a young man or woman must find a place offers a certain ideal of man; and every civilization tends to present that ideal as an absolute value with respect to the principles or conventions that gave birth to it.

Certainly, it would be naïve for us to believe that history consists of a series of great leaps forward, interrupted by periods of uneventful calm. Even so, it is not entirely wrong to say that, so far as youth's search for moral integration into society is concerned, the present era is characterized by a universal and disturbing questioning of the whole of civilization. Until a half century ago, despite wars and social convulsions, young people generally prepared to enter a world that was relatively stable. Today, however, civilization itself, rather than certain aspects of civilization, is regarded as unstable—and unstable to a point where modern man is brought face to face with the most relentless mysteries of human destiny, to a greater degree perhaps than ever before in human history. "Unstable youth" perceives itself as confronting a world that is itself unstable; and therein, no doubt, lies the wholly new phenomenon that forces us to reflect deeply on the very foundations of morality.

In May 1968, there occurred the student uprisings in Paris. This upheaval, whether implicitly or explicitly, was a dramatic manifestation of a materialistic concept of man

and his destiny; and it makes no difference at all whether
that concept found its inspiration in capitalism or in Marxism. From that event, we can draw the conclusion that a
young man, of, say, eighteen years, today does not know in
what sort of world he will spend his life. During a debate
that followed a meeting in a French city, a seventy-year-old
professor of literature, with the best of intentions, and filled
with love for young people, complained that youth was unable to say what it was that they wanted. "We are ready to
give you whatever you want," he said, "but you must at
least tell us what it is you want. Tell us what you want us
to do." A young man of eighteen or nineteen answered,
explaining calmly that the professor had put his finger on
the problem: that the reason for unrest among young people was that they were unable to express concretely, even
to themselves, their desires and plans with respect to what
might be called the collapse of civilization. He concluded
with this remark, which requires no explanation: "What we
are asking adults to do is simply this: to respect our uncertainty."

In a way, we can say that adolescence and youth are,
for every human subject, the time during which he becomes
aware of the fundamental uncertainty that characterizes
human nature. From another aspect, we can say also that
the era in which we are living, with its "breakdown of
civilization," constitutes the recognition of a fundamental
insecurity. It is not surprising that that insecurity is sometimes expressed by explosions of aggression in the search for
something new.

As we have said before, from the standpoint of modern
anthropology, man is defined by means of an essential and

congenital uncertainty. Unlike other animals, man is not guided by instinct; that is, man must create his own activities, his own meaning, and his own adjustments. In other words, the specific difference of man is *insecurity.* We never know if a chosen course of conduct is perfectly compatible with the more or less conscious needs that motivate it. Whether we are talking about individual or collective behavior, the essentially dominant factor—which is never resolved—is that of uncertainty and insecurity. This insecurity may be more or less conscious, individual or collective; but it remains radical in every instance.

It is not surprising, surely, that mankind has always tried to resolve that insecurity, and often to camouflage it. It is precisely because of this fundamental insecurity that the world today is subjected to a phenomenon that is as all-pervasive as it is wholly new, at least in its larger aspects. It is always dangerous, of course, to resort to simplifications of history. Still, we can say that, on the whole, up to the present age, mankind spontaneously looked for the solution to its insecurity in another world, or in an imaginary being that was the product of human uncertainty; that is, in a "divinity" that was presented as possessing all knowledge and having the answer to the ultimate enigma. This being, whom we may call the Supposedly Knowing Subject, since he possessed all knowledge, also disposed of all power.

The Supposedly Knowing Subject has taken a thousand forms in history, from the most totemic deities to the monotheistic elaborations that occurred from time to time in the Egypt of the pharaohs. But, whatever its form, whether single or multiple, magical or mythological, and

to whatever degree modified in its structure by metaphysical factors, this divinity was always regarded and treated
as the Supposedly Knowing Subject; and thus, it was the
divinity who was the final arbiter of human behavior down
to the smallest detail.[1]

At the dawn of the modern era, however, a change
occurred in human thought; something new and strange
appeared. Up until then, when a man wanted to achieve
knowledge, to penetrate the secrets of nature, he generally
asked questions, in one way or another, of the Supposedly
Knowing Being. By means of magic, the wisdom of the
ancients, metaphysics and theology, or by certain behavioral rituals, this Being was thought to be induced to share
with mankind some bits of knowledge. The new way of
doing things became clearly evident in the seventeenth
century. It did not happen all at once, of course; it was
preceded by at least a century of thought and reflection.
What is most striking, however, is that this new human
attitude toward knowledge—which may be described as
a properly scientific attitude—was implicit in all striving
after knowledge for a thousand years before, without being
clearly perceived or taken into account. It was not until
the seventeenth century that this phenomenon, and this
attitude, was clearly manifested in such a way as to transform completely man's intellectual life.

The man who, among others, articulated this attitude

[1] It is interesting to note in passing that what is revealed in the Bible,
in a progressive and complex manner, is not a divinity that is a Supposedly
Knowing Subject, but a *Savior*.

Translator's Note: The term used by the author is *Sujet Supposé
Savoir*—"the subject who is commonly believed to know" or "the subject who is supposed to know."

was René Descartes; and those who lived it in the reality of their thought were such men as Pascal, Galileo, and many others. From that time forward, when men wished to understand "the secrets of nature," to acquire the elements of knowledge that would enable them to lead a better life, they no longer addressed themselves to the Supposedly Knowing Subject; instead, they abstracted from that Subject, and set about searching for knowledge on their own. Thus, science rid itself once and for all of its magical, metaphysical and theological context, acquired an identity of its own, and became a specifically human activity. This transformation has far-reaching implications in man's quest for the solution to human insecurity, and has consequences that are more profound than we are now capable of realizing.

It is almost axiomatic that there is much less difference between twelfth-century man and seventeenth-century man than between the latter and twentieth-century man. If one were required to synopsize this development in very few words, it would not be altogether incorrect to say that the modern world has been thoroughly "demythologized." We no longer attribute to a divinity, whatever that divinity's name, those phenomena that we understand and of which we know the cause and the mechanics (which is not to say that we know *ultimate* causes, or that we understand anything in all its ramifications). This demythologizing process affected, first, the forces of nature; then, the living world, and especially the animal world; and, finally, in our own time—especially since the appearance of psychoanalysis—man himself and the human mechanism.

At about the same time, especially since the middle of

the nineteenth century, man began to be aware of the essential evolutional and dynamic nature of the universe, including the human universe. This is the whole meaning, for example, of the work of Teilhard de Chardin. History itself has been demythologized. Certainly, history is not an exact science in the way that, say, mathematics is an exact science; it is, nonetheless, a science—that is, a body of knowledge accumulated solely by human resources.[2]

As far as morality is concerned, the result of this change in attitude is as evident as it is disconcerting. If man is to resolve his basic insecurity, where is he to find the authoritative knowledge that he needs? The Supposedly Knowing Subject, having been demythologized, no longer enjoys the absolute, sovereign, and transcendent authority that once was a sure guide through the complexities of human behavior. And that is perhaps the most important point in what is happening in today's world: the "divinity" is now perceived as a figment of the imagination, and is no longer regarded as possessing the secret of knowledge as far as human deportment is concerned. The Supposedly Knowing Subject is no longer the dictator of moral standards.

This may seem a strange statement from a man who regards himself as a convinced Christian, and who believes with all his heart in the mystery of Christ. But that is the core of the problem. Contemporary man cannot accept the mystery of Christ, which is absolutely central to his

[2] The process of demythologization has not spared, obviously, those historical documents dealing with the life of Jesus. It is worth remarking that the more scientific knowledge increases and is consolidated, the more the boundaries of the incomprehensible are simultaneously restricted and better defined. This, however, is another problem, and one that it is not the purpose of this chapter to discuss.

existence, in the guise of a Supposedly Knowing Subject from the prescientific age. When we say, "God is dead," we are perfectly correct, for a certain concept of the divinity, given the scientific knowledge at our disposal, is no longer valid. What we often forget, however, is that this same scientific knowledge raises a question without an answer that is more profound and much more urgent than any ever raised before.

Regarding moral standards, therefore, modern man is thrown back on his own resources. He must somehow find, within himself and by his own efforts, by reflecting on his ideals and his limitations, the meaning of human dynamism and human autonomy. He can no longer depend upon a Supposedly Knowing Subject. He must now live with the sometimes intolerable necessity of discovering by himself what he must do. Obviously, this does not solve the problem of human uncertainty; but it does put it in a new light. Without oversimplifying matters, we could say that modern man finds himself in a situation comparable to that of the adolescent with respect to adults. The adolescent must establish his identity for himself; but this does not mean that he must do away with the adult world simply because his relation to that world has changed. Mankind is in the same position with respect to the Supposedly Knowing Subject, in that he will not tolerate the Subject's interference in his quest for autonomy. But this hardly means that man must discard, or is rejecting, the true mystery of a Being who exists within a plan that man must henceforth perceive in a totally new and different way.

A child regards an adult as an all-knowing being, and fashions his behavior according to the dictates of that

adult—that is, according to *law*. Until modern times, man
lived in the same way with respect to the *law* that was supposed to express the will of the Supposedly Knowing Subject. It is strange, nonetheless, that for two thousand years
a puzzling passage from St. Paul[3] on the question has been
so often ignored or misconstrued. It is a disturbing passage
and a particularly relevant one today. Even if law is necessary for the moral guidance of a man, or of mankind, it
seems that it is essentially inadequate, and that it even
becomes an obstacle when it is regarded as the final word
in morality. And this, of course, is what is wrong with a
strictly legalistic approach to morality. It is hardly necessary to point out that the moral crisis among young people
is precisely that they reject, absolutely and sometimes
aggressively, morality by edict. In all scientific honesty,
we must recognize that this rejection is the reflex of a
healthy mind and the result of a search for humanization.
The meaning of human acts, the complexion of human
morality, the exigencies of the dynamics of human behavior—all these things must be sought by man within
man. And this, quite evidently, represents a radical change
in our concept of authority (or of law) at every level of
human life.

Until modern times, the quest for knowledge was rather
like a relay race. The Supposedly Knowing Subject passed
on a part of his secret knowledge to the representative of
divine authority on earth—the king or the priest. The king
and the priest were in direct contact with the divinity, a
relationship which distinguished them from the rest of
mankind. Now that the Supposedly Knowing Subject has

[3] Romans, 7. See appendix for full text of this passage.

been evicted by modern research, it follows that, in the process, the king and the priest have also been stripped of a function that was, in effect, a myth. The king and the priest are now no more than other men; they have no access to secret knowledge; like all men, they must live with the uncertainty and ambiguity of man's search for truth. There can be no more representative of a Supposedly Knowing Subject. In fact, today the mysteries of the universe can be perceived only under a completely different aspect from that of the Supposedly Knowing Subject. The professor of moral theology can no longer be the source of our knowledge on how we must live, for the simple reason that a professor of moral theology is now seen for what he is: a man like other men, searching like other men, and sharing the uncertainties and frustrations of those whom he is supposed to teach. Within that context, the *law*, whether we mean a fundamental law or a positive law evolved to respond to a social need, is no longer regarded as an end in itself. Instead, it represents the result of a common effort, and a statement of a common viewpoint, which is intended to become a meeting ground for the common elaboration of something else. From that perspective, a person in authority is seen as a delegate of the rest of mankind in the search for knowledge. His role is, by participating in that search, to guide it, and to assume the same posture as all other men *vis à vis* the question without answer that is the mystery of human destiny.

2. MORALITY—
AN UNCERTAIN SCIENCE

It was not very long ago that what we call the "human sciences" first appeared. (In fact, one of the most noteworthy things about scientific progress is that man has had to wait almost until our own time to become the object of the scientific attitude that he articulated and developed since the seventeenth century.) These human sciences are both complex and varied; and we should say at the beginning that we are not talking about *exact sciences* in the mathematical sense of that term, but about disciplines that are, nonetheless, sciences. Generally speaking, we can divide such sciences into three categories: first, physiology and biology; second, psychology (since the time of Freud); and, finally, sociology and psychosociology. From these disciplines as a whole, there is emerging, at the present time, a global view of man which is very different from that which obtained in the prescientific era.

One datum of that view is that the human race is specifically characterized—that is, distinguished from other

living beings—by its basic and congenital lack of adjustment to its future existence. This nonadjustment is at once
individual and collective. Human young go out into the
world totally unprepared for life; they enter a life situation completely different from that which they have known.
The young of animals, on the other hand, seem somehow
adjusted to the exigencies and needs of their lives, and
they behave *instinctively* in accordance with those needs.
They are, as it were, preadjusted to their lives. Thus, living
beings make up a dynamic whole that seems well organ-
ized and well adjusted, and which exists in a state that we
call "natural." Out of that natural state, however, has
sprung up a new being, man, who seems to have made his
appearance progressively, albeit rapidly, a million or a
million and a half years ago. In this human race, instinct,
which is so well regulated in other animals, seems somehow
deficient, or essentially inadequate. Man is, as the French
writer Vercors pointed out, "a denatured animal."

This deficiency of instinct has far-reaching consequences as far as the way that man lives is concerned. If an
animal is perfectly, or almost perfectly, adjusted to one
sort of behavioral pattern, then that pattern hardly ever
varies. Therefore, behavior among animals—even domestic or trained animals—is largely stereotyped. The best
example of this behavioral invariability is that of a shep-
herd dog who is trained by his master to lead a herd of
cattle to drink from a nearby river. During a drought,
when the river dries up and the cattle have to be taken to
a spring, which is farther away, the dog will insist on leading the herd to the dried-up river, and will not allow them

to go to the spring. We are occasionally moved by stories of domestic animals (dogs, especially) who "let themselves die of hunger" on the graves of their masters. What their death means, in fact, is that they were aware of no behavioral alternative; their behavior was so narrowly conditioned that they were unable to adjust to a new way of life. It is only man who is subject to that fundamental lack of precision which results in the possibility of behavioral adjustment; which means that there exists for man a spectrum of possible adjustments. Man, it appears, is forced by his neurophysiological conditioning to invent. His range of experiences, experiments, and adjustments is truly limitless. For the truth of this statement to appear, we have only to reflect for a moment on the incredible diversity of human habitations, as compared to the invariability of the dens of animals of the same species.

As far as man's adjustment to and development in his existence is concerned, this means that man is free of compulsion with respect to his environment and to his behavior in relation to his environment. He is not a part of nature in the same way animals are. Freud's discovery of the emotional evolution of the human personality, beginning in earliest childhood, demonstrates this conclusively. The infant, in confrontation with the human beings surrounding him, begins immediately to look for a way to behave so as to assure that his relations with them will be harmonious and satisfactory. Certainly, in the first few months of life, that search is not conscious; nonetheless, it involves, as psychoanalysis shows, certain unconscious and very primitive representations that are called "phantasms." These primitive representations are the basic conditioning that allow for later development. Slowly and progressively, we see the child become aware of himself; he reflects, questions, as though experiencing a certain sense of autonomy with respect to his environment, and above all with respect to the other humans in that environment. This, in the simplest terms, constitutes the progressive emergence of what is called "awareness." This awareness is, in reality, a quest. Whether we are talking about mankind in a collective sense, or about the conscious emotional evolution of an individual subject, it remains true that this quest is continual—and continually unsatisfied in the final analysis—and that it results, at the level of civilization, in that essentially human phenomenon that we call "culture." Animals do not have to search in order to live; but man's life is a perennial search, and one that is never ended. Basically, the entire human condition may be summed up in one question: What must we do in order to live a better life? Here we are in the dimension of *desire,* which translates and introduces into behavior the perception (never resolved, and never ceasing) of a *lack;* that is, of a distance from one's environment, of an endless search for one's proper place. In other words, a human being, compared to an animal, is *obliged* by his very nature to control his own behavior and to be constantly in search of a better means of adjustment. To put it more simply, man, as distinguished from the infinitely complex world, both animate and inanimate, from which he springs, is a moral being.

We have often used the words "search" and "quest." What, exactly, is it that man is looking for? We may say that man is searching for a means to relieve a perpetually recurring tension between human awareness and man's environment. The at least temporary resolution of this tension is called, in Freudian terminology, *pleasure,* in the broadest meaning of the word. This, I think, is the basic meaning of the psychoanalytic concept of the *libido;* i.e., the desire for pleasure insofar as it resolves man's fundamental nonadjustment. The sexual aspect of this problem is, in fact, probably only the most intense and immediately perceptible manifestation of it.

Man, since he exists in a state of perpetual and un- resolved nonadjustment, constantly seeks to adjust; that is, to develop and satisfy his deepest needs, even though such needs may be perceived only confusedly. (And this obscure perception, of course, does not simplify matters.) What this means, in the simplest possible terms—and at the risk of seeming absurdly banal—is that the whole of human existence consists in the search for happiness. Every effort at moral reflection, every casting about for standards of conduct, all "laws," all philosophical observations on human deportment—everything is aimed at discovering the road to happiness.

It is important, even though some may find it unexpected, to note that such a man as Thomas Aquinas—a true man of the Middle Ages—said exactly the same thing in other terms. In fact, in the Third Part of the *Summa,* he began his treatise on moral theology by a discussion of happiness. For Aquinas, every moral quest was a quest for happiness—it being understood that happiness must be situated at its proper (transcendental) level. Yet the fact remains that, ultimately, every moral quest lies at that same level. If we approach this body of reflections without semantic prejudice, we may interpret it as follows: the human race, since its beginning—and each of us as individuals, since our birth—is constantly seeking to learn how we must act in order to attain perfect happiness. And therein lies the deepest meaning of morality. It is not a question of *observing* a law, but of making use of the implications of a law in order to aim, individually and collectively, at the attainment of that perfect happiness which is the essential motivation, and the final secret, of human dynamics.

The only problem, and the one to which there is no answer, is that this quest after happiness will never be fully and perfectly satisfied.

The essential date of modern psychology on this question, inaugurated by the discoveries of Freud, may be expressed in this way: man essentially seeks, in both his individual and collective relations, to attain a situation in which everyone is recognized by everyone else as an individual, and a fully subjective individual. In other words, what motivates the search for behavioral norms—that is, the search for a moral code—is the fundamental need for the full and final success of *love*.

As it happens, however, this is the question to which no science can give the answer. For man, despite his constant seeking, does not attain that success.

What can man do about this situation? Why is it that man is essentially incapable of achieving the full expression of himself? These are the only two important questions in matters of morality. It seems that in today's world, because of the collective and progressive increase in awareness brought about by a scientific civilization, these are also the two main points of questioning among young peo- ple. That is, What must a man do in order to become more fully a man? And, Why is it that he does not succeed in this attempt?

3. FALSE VALUES

Mankind, in its eternal search for an ideal of behavior capable of conferring happiness—i.e., capable of banishing man's fundamental insecurity—has sought, through a diversity of cultures and over thousands of years, to lay down certain points of reference, certain principles, certain "values" to guide him in that search. It now seems that one of the most important aspects of the present moral crisis is that these traditional values, once regarded as enduring, if not immutable, have been demythologized—or, if you prefer, debunked. This, very likely, is the reason behind the current hostility directed against what is called "middle-class morality." If we accept that term at more than face value, we may conclude that what is being contested is the pretension that many of the traditions and rules engender a sense of security, while in fact they have been shown to be ineffectual in the present situation. The awareness of this deficiency in traditional moral standards is perhaps often implicit; but it is beyond debate that it has, on certain occasions, been very explicit, and that, in the heat of battle, it has been demonstrated enthusiastically, and even methodically. Among the so-called values proposed by this middle-class morality, and certainly among those being challenged by young people are money, technological progress, the cult of comfort, and also something that one might call "socialist idealism."

Money, the first of these contested values, is the most obvious target of young people's disaffection. It is a commonplace truth that money does not make happiness. And yet, we somehow manage to slip around the evidence supporting that assertion, to disguise it, or even to deny it. Jean Fourastié, in his *Morale prospective,* shows to what degree the customs, life-style, and general dynamics of behavior among the governing classes at the turn of the century were profoundly and openly dictated by the semblance of security conferred by material possessions. There are many cruel pages in Fourastié's work about the behavior and the values of the generation in question. (It is interesting to note that Fourastié is no more gentle in his last novel, when he speaks of the tyranny implicit in the ownership of land.)

Admitting that possession is one of the fundamental needs of human existence, it is possible, if not probable, that young people today have become aware that possession in itself, regardless of what it is that is possessed, is not the key to the attainment of happiness. The ownership of land, of money, of objects that have monetary value, serves to disguise, and sometimes to aggravate, man's agonizing lack of certainty—his awareness of the fact that he lacks something. Possession of anything cannot be a moral value in the strict sense of the term; and this is something that we recognize almost intuitively, and most disturbingly, in the modern world.

The relationship of the possessor to that which is possessed is essentially limited, and thus unsatisfying; for that which is possessed always retains a certain degree of freedom. For example, if I contemplate a Rembrandt painting in a museum, I have every right to enjoy and to profit from Rembrandt's artistic genius, and even from the mystery of Rembrandt's personality, which is expressed in the painting. There is nothing to prevent me from establishing a relationship of knowledge and understanding, not only with the object itself but also with the man who effected it and who communicates with me through the object. The contemplation of this work of art, which I do not *own*, leaves me completely free to learn as much as possible from it. If, on the other hand, I have a Rembrandt hanging in my living room, this freedom, this wealth of relationships, will be limited, and perhaps seriously hindered, by another factor, by an inevitable attitude on my part that will interfere with my enjoyment even without my being aware of it. In such a situation, there are two things that will appear: first, the satisfaction that I derive is not solely from the quality of the painting itself, but from the knowledge that the painting is *mine;* and, second, the fear that, somehow, I may lose possession of the painting. It is no exaggeration, therefore, to say that, in this case, possession deprives me of the intellectual liberty to enjoy the painting in all its glory by preventing me from giving myself over wholly to its enjoyment. Thus, I profit less from the painting than I would if I did not own it.

Within the same context, we may say that the expression "private property" is a misstatement of fact. What we call "private property" is, in effect, "depriving property." In the case of the Rembrandt painting hanging on my wall, I am depriving other people of its enjoyment; an enjoyment that would be theirs if the painting were hanging in a museum and were not my property. In owning *my* Rembrandt, I am depriving others of it. My ownership may be a source of aggressive and rather bitter satisfaction to me—a sort of revenge against mankind, or a compensation for a sense of inferiority in another area. But it may also be a source of suffering to me if I stop to think about it; for the painting is so incredibly beautiful that it may pain me to think that I would enjoy it even more if everyone could see it and share it with me, if I could discuss it with art lovers, if more people could profit from it.

The question of "depriving property" is a very complicated one. Possession is a fundamental requirement of existence and of survival. It is easy not to feel too guilty about owning a Rembrandt and thus depriving other people of it. But what if we are talking about a bed that I am depriving someone of? Sleep is absolutely essential, and so I must have a bed, a bed that no one else has the use of. It should not worry me, particularly, that my ownership of this particular bed is depriving someone else of it. After all, my need to sleep is as absolute as anyone else's. In the same way, no one else can physically sit down in the same chair that I occupy. Within that context, it becomes clear that there are certain things the ownership of which is absolutely necessary—those things that enable me to survive independently and ensure me a minimum of self-respect. But where does this absolutely necessary owner-ship stop, and where does "depriving property"—that is, aggressive ownership, directed against other human beings —start? The problem is infinitely complex, infinitely variable, and quite impossible to solve by means of any sort of absolute or fixed criteria. And this lack of criteria, of course, contributes largely to the insecurity that we are always trying to allay.

One summer several years ago, I was in Avignon for that city's annual festival. The place was packed with the usual collection of tourists, jet-setters and young people. In the main square, a group of hippies of both sexes were engaged in various business activities—some of them were selling "art," and others were panhandling. I recall particularly a young girl, in ragged clothing, who sat on the ground, begging. She had written, in chalk, something like this: "There are works of art, ceramics, reproductions, etc., for sale in this city. I would like to look at them, and to own some of them. But, because of the kind of consumer society in which we live, I will have to pay for them." And under the poster was a cup for donations.

I stood watching the girl for a few minutes. She noticed me, and asked me for a donation. I refused. I was tempted to take the chalk, which was still lying there, and add this sentence to what she had written: "Unfortunately, I have to pay too." What particularly disturbed me about this girl's plea for contributions was that it was an obvious and aggressive claim *against* a certain kind of society, and that it was also, at the same time—no doubt, without the girl's being aware of it—a claim based *on* the kind of

society that she was supposedly rejecting; that is, on a
society that valued the concept of "depriving property"—
that is, of ownership that was directed against others
and that shut out other people. She wanted to *own* the
things that she was begging money to buy. (Moreover,
from the tone of the chalked words, it was obvious that she
considered all passersby to be either imbeciles, or bour-
geoisie, or both. If I can bring myself to believe that I am
not actually an imbecile, and that I am not bourgeois in
the sense that she gave the term, I do not see how I could
put any money in her cup.) Abstracting from this contradiction, however, it is clear what the girl's sentiments were:
she was registering, perhaps without realizing it, a strong
and dramatic protest against the division of wealth that
characterizes our society—a division that is essentially
unjust and unacceptable precisely because it exalts the possession of material goods.

A relationship based upon possession is limiting both
for the owner and for other people. What is owned is always *a thing,* and so it is, by its nature, a limited thing.
It is not a paradox to say that the more things that one
owns for oneself, and the more other people are deprived
of those things, the more the things that one owns are
limited. Let me give one example. If I want to own a field,
or a part of a field, in order to raise vegetables, I must first
of all post the part that I want to use; that is, I must forbid
anyone other than myself to use this piece of land, or even
to set foot on it. In other words, people now can use only
that part that I have not fenced in—a reduced and limited
part of the field as a whole. This is a purely symbolic example, but it serves to illustrate, I think, to what extent

material objects—land, money, etc.—are the cause of litigation, rivalry, confrontations, conflicts, dissatisfaction, and war.

In reading over the preceding paragraphs, it strikes me that I am beating a dead horse. The ills caused by ownership are known to everyone. There is even a French axiom to express it: *La propriété, c'est le vol*—"Property is robbery." No doubt, this saying is related to one that I mentioned earlier: "Money does not make for happiness." The fact is, money docs not make for the happiness of the one who owns the money. It positively makes for unhappiness among those who do not have enough money because of those who have too much of it—and therein lies the robbery.

A certain Jesus of Nazareth observed once that no man can serve both God and Mammon . . .

Young people today, caught up in the trauma of a civilization in dramatic evolution, are certainly more aware than ever that possession—even *necessary* possession—is the source of aggression and unhappiness, and that it impedes rather than furthers the quest for security.

Possession, in short, is a false value. When youth revolts against what it calls, generally, the "consumer society," it is probably not revolting directly against society itself, but against the great, unanswered needs that exist within that society. In other words, it is not against society that young people are revolting, but against the goals of that society. It is those goals, rather than society itself, that alienate today's youth. Obviously, this is not always explicit, not even most of the time. Even so, we must recognize the fact that man's desire for exclusive possession becomes literally intolerable at a certain point—perhaps because the desire to possess something at any price reveals, ultimately, the basic inanity of a system that makes a value of possession.

The enormous advances in science and technology made during the past century and a half have created a gap between man and his environment. Man is no longer in contact with "nature." One of the consequences of this loss of contact is that man has become aware, as never before, that technology of any kind has no moral value as such. It may have a technical value, according to whether or not it is effective; but it has no direct connection with moral values—that is, with the meaning of existence. In other words, technology is neither good nor bad; it is only the uses made of technology that are good or bad.

There used to be—and there still is, often—a concept of nature that regarded nature as a sort of personalized intermediary deity. One was not allowed to act "against nature," or to "contradict nature." It is because of this concept of nature that the progress of science and technology has led to a new and very deep attitude of questioning. We can say that, over all, man now realizes that nature-as-a-deity does not exist. Nature exists only as an area to be explored, to be used in such a way as to further man's search for security and to guide man in that search. Events at the human level are not the same as events at other levels in the universe. Man questions, and he searches beyond nature for the proper path for humanity and for his own destiny. This is almost self-evident to the contemporary mind; but it is a comparatively new truth, and one that perhaps is not universally accepted.

Technology is simply the means of discovering how to use something that has been found in nature. The moral problem of technology lies in the phrase "how to use." A technological application is good to the degree that it is in conformity with the scientific data on which it is based. In the same way, it is good if it accomplishes, concretely and immediately, what it was intended to do. For example, a knife is good if it cuts well. This has not the slightest moral implication. At another level, if I use that knife to carve a roast for my dinner guests, I am making good use of it. If, on the other hand, I make use of this good—i.e., sharp—knife to murder someone, I am making a bad use of it. In the latter case, the knife is still good, but *I* am bad, and I am making a bad use of a good thing.

At first glance, the reasoning outlined above is so elementary as to be obvious. And yet this is precisely the problem that is raised when it comes to the question of contraceptives. Sexual morality will be discussed in a later chapter; but it would be helpful to note here that the crux of the debate stirred up by the encyclical *Humanae vitae* is the belief that a technological application, or a technique, of itself is morally indifferent. For some reason, when sexual morality is discussed, some people still fall back on the concept of nature-as-a-deity and talk about a chemical or a mechanical device as being "against nature." The question is this: Is a contraceptive technique good, or is it bad? For the answer, we may refer to what we said about the knife. A contraceptive technique is good if it prevents impregnation, if it does not harm the user, if it is not detrimental to the good of the family, and if its effect is only temporary. At this point, however, the moral problem begins: how, and in what spirit, does one make use of contraceptives?

That is a rather uncomfortable question. It is much easier, and gives a much greater feeling of security, to follow blindly the laws of so-called nature, than to be compelled constantly to search, to improvise, to be responsible for one's own decisions, to be eternally questioning one's own judgment and values. It is not impossible that those who invoke nature are reacting almost instinctively to man's primitive need for security.

The problem of birth control illustrates very well the basic problem of man's search for moral standards. This problem may be stated briefly as follows: until modern times, the rate of infant mortality (i.e., during infancy or early childhood) was about 70 percent. Obviously, the idea that it might be necessary to limit the number of births did not occur to anyone. Now, however, scientific progress and its technological application in the areas of biology, pathology, hygiene, etc., have drastically reduced the infant mortality rate to an average, in the industrial nations of the world, of 1.5 percent. A triumph, surely, of human progress. At the same time, a new problem has arisen; a problem, judging by the public discussion of it, of which the whole world is aware: that of imminent overpopulation, either at the family level or at the infinitely more complex level of population growth in relation to new research and new discoveries in the field of birth-control methods; that is, in ways of imposing reasonable limitations on population growth. Such discoveries have been particularly spectacular in hormonal studies and in the means of controlling ovarian functions, and they have led to the development and dissemination of contraceptive means that, as techniques, are *good*. Here, however, the same problem as that posed by the knife must intrude: how, and for what purpose, should one make use of these *good* techniques?

This question cannot be answered without a step forward in the study of human behavior in general, and of human sexuality in particular. It would appear, for example, that human sexuality, while it is a factor in reproduction of the species (as it is among all animals) is, at the same time, something more than that—something that affects the very essence of man and to which we have not devoted a great deal of thought. To put it in the form of a question: Is it possible that human sexuality, when it is exercised independently and distinctly from its reproductive function, has a *relational* value of prime importance? Technological progress, while it helps us to understand the question with greater clarity than before, cannot provide the answer. A moral answer cannot be found at the level of the intrinsic quality of a technique, for at that level we find new questions and new problems of morality rather than solutions and answers. Such questions and problems represent progress, it is true; but they also contribute to human insecurity and doubt. Techniques are merely techniques; that is, they can answer no questions about the value or meaning of human behavior. Even worse, these techniques are themselves deeply ambivalent as far as their results are concerned, because, in addition to the problems they raise, they reveal the fundamental uncertainty and congenital insecurity of mankind.

Perhaps the most striking example of this lies in the field

of communications, the area in which modern civilization differs most from that of former centuries. The present-day emphasis upon communications no doubt reflects a widespread desire to understand other men and to arrive at a certain human consensus that we can call "peace." At the same time, however, we are presented simultaneously with the extraordinary phenomenon of the President of the United States being able to converse with American astronauts on the moon—and with that of neighboring human communities being apparently unable to understand one another's thoughts or aspirations. In Ireland, for instance, most people have radios, television sets, and telephones. This represents a recognition of the fact that human language is a means of specific intersubjective communication. And yet this very same language, at the same time, is used to communicate the news that men are unable to communicate with each other. And even this inability to communicate is perceived by those concerned as incommunicable.

Since the time of Freud, almost everyone knows that there is a part of us that eludes our conscious mind, and that this incommunicability of what is communicable exists in every one of us. When I explain to someone what is on my mind, I can see that, at best, he only half-understands me, and that I myself do not really understand all that I am saying. This results, among other things, in a disquieting realization that I am at least partly incomprehensible, even to myself.

The lesson to be drawn from this is that technology, while it is indicative of increased knowledge and the increased mastery by man of his environment, reveals to man that technological progress is not, of itself, the means of finding an answer to the riddle of man. To the contrary, technology only emphasizes the reality of that riddle.

The corollary of this awareness regarding the ultimate significance of technological progress is that the indisputable (albeit ambivalent) benefits derived from such progress do not constitute the goal of the human quest. Going a step further, we may say that technological progress only serves to make it brutally clear that there are areas inaccessible to man, and that man is incapable of finding the final solution to his problem.

It seems to me that the hippie phenomenon and that of the drug culture are striking symptoms of the contemporary world's realization of that disconcerting truth.

I do not know whether, from the standpoint of economics, the observations that follow are valid; I do know, however, that from the viewpoint of psychology and of life they are perfectly true.

Having covered myself, let me define our "consumer society" as an at least implicit collective experience of unbounded plenty and unlimited contentment based upon technological progress and upon what we may call the concept of *comfort*. This is to say that the direction in which our civilization is evolving is based upon the assumption that a solution will be found to every problem, and that, once all our problems and uncertainties are thus resolved, we will be happy. Without exaggerating, we can say that, in this collective attitude, society represents an unconscious mother-image. That is, the mother is regarded as the source and giver of all security and all contentment, independently of any initiative on the child's part. It is possible that this analogy explains one of the basic reasons for youth's alienation and rebellion in the contemporary world; perhaps young people are not revolting against the mother-image so much as they are rebelling against the need that they feel for a mother-image.

We have said that the happiness and satisfactions derived from technological progress do not lessen man's basic insecurity. It is nonetheless true—and this may be what is happening today—that this technological perfection can serve to disguise that insecurity. In such a case, there appears a symptom characteristic of our culture in general, and especially characteristic of America, where that culture exists in its most developed form; and that characteristic is, simply, an all-pervasive sense of boredom. Apparently, all of man's problems have been solved, or will be solved, by perfecting the telephone, the refrigerator, or the automobile. It is, then, as though the human unrest that rises up from deep within us has nothing to which to attach itself; as though the fundamental aggressiveness of man, which tends to compensate for man's fundamental *lack,* now has no real target. In more simple terms, the apparent success of technological socialized civilization leads to an even more disturbing question than before, for man is saying today: "If all of *this* is not solving our problems, then what is left for us to do?" The failing of a technological civilization is precisely that it confuses man concerning what he must fight against if he is to survive. And that is by no means a paradox.

It has been observed clinically, and the datum has often been published and discussed, that, between 1939 and

1946, despite especially inadequate facilities for treatment, the incidence of alcoholism fell drastically. The reason for this drop is that alcohol is a stimulant, albeit a mild one. A film producer explained it to me in this way after he had completed a film on the Resistance: "When we were young during the war, we fought for something that was tremendously important to us. We had no need, and no time, for such things as marijuana. . . ." In other words, fighters in the French Resistance had no need for alcohol or drugs or other stimulants; they were stimulated enough by their ideals. Within that context, the hippie phenomenon, like the drug phenomenon, is nothing more, so to speak, than a collective and alarming flight, inspired by despair, toward an imaginary world. How is it that a civilization founded upon hope can end up in despair and in boredom? How is it, in other words, that we are no longer stimulated by our ideals? The more we reflect on the events of the past few years, the more we realize that this is the basic question. It is, in any case, the question that the younger generation is asking, either implicitly or explicitly. It would be useless and wrong to ask who is responsible for this situation. No one is at fault; or, in another sense, everyone is at fault—which comes to the same thing. For that matter, the question of individual responsibility is not the most important one, or the most difficult to answer. What we can state, however, in a general way, is that today the pursuit of *comfort* and the pleasures conferred by a consumer society cannot be regarded as moral values for the young people just beginning their lives. They already know all too well, from sad experience, about this comfort and these pleasures.

Progress, in the broadest sense of the term, which aims at the improvement of human existence and at the ideal solution of all human problems, is essentially ambivalent; and this ambivalence is without a solution. On the one hand, it is *good,* since it has a humanizing tendency and promotes the dignity and freedom of man. On the other hand, it simultaneously and eventually leads to results that, in the present situation, are directly contrary to dignity and freedom. Humanization remains in the realm of ideas as far as the modern world is concerned—as demonstrated by the wars and other atrocities that are the reality of everyday life. And, as far as human dignity is concerned, it is sufficient to observe how technological progress has led to a modern form of slavery for certain classes of working people—a form even more revolting than the official slavery of other days.

Progress as such, therefore, is obviously incapable of making man happy, and it can be no more than a *relative* moral value. This fact brings us to the question to which man, left to himself, can find no answer: What went wrong in our search for happiness and progress? Why is it that we have found just the opposite of what we were seeking?

The term "socialism" is one of the most equivocal words in the language. If by it we mean a methodical social system that, as distinguished from capitalism as it actually exists, aims at avoiding oppression of one class by another, then we are obviously talking about something very desirable, and we can say that socialism has a very positive moral value. But if we mean a system that, by whatever economic, political, and social means, is supposed to result eventually in an absolutely ideal and perfect human society, then socialism is a utopian dream. And we might note in passing, however disagreeable it may be, that utopia consists in the illusion that something is possible which is, in fact, absolutely impossible. Utopias are the most dangerous of all excuses for a flight from the mysterious reality of things. And it seems—especially in France since May and June 1968—that collectively, the young people of our time have recognized this latter form of socialism for what it is, and have rejected its utopian ideal as such, even though they may see, in its internal dynamism, a very real factor in the search for humanization and for moral strength. It is precisely because it is utopian that they have rejected it; just as they have rejected the static and stagnant image of the so-called bourgeois society, and just as they reject (inasmuch as they are its first citizens) the consumer society, the technological and comfortable society into which they were born through no choice of their own.

The upheavals of May and June 1968 were contemporary youth's expression of its urgent need to discover the meaning of existence. I do not think that this need can be satisfied by a mere occupational and social adjustment to life as it is now or as it will be. The question that young people are asking goes much deeper than that. It is striking that the May-June uprising was aimed equally at what we can call the surviving elements of "ecclesiastical Christianity" and at what can also be called "the communist church," which has solidified into its own illusions, dogmas, and hierarchy. It is perhaps a sign also of this same insistent questioning that young people everywhere were united by a feeling of the most intense sympathy for the people of

Prague on the occasion of that city's revolt against foreign domination, and during the repression of that revolt.

The moral dogmatism that dominated Western civilization during the nineteenth century, and the dogmatism of communism, are equally stifling and equally intolerable. Both schools of thought violate and oppress human freedom instead of promoting it within an interrelational whole, although the means that they use to do so are at least superficially different. In effect, these two concepts of human society, despite the fact that they are based upon different promises, both tend to subordinate individual aspirations and ideals to a certain collective ideal. This, of course, is nothing more than a statement of the eternal conflict between the life of the community as a whole and that of the individuals within that community; and it would literally be childish to believe, given the realities of human existence, that this conflict will one day admit of a solution.

If a civilization based upon progress—that is, upon both technological advances and upon the humanizing progress that may accompany those advances—can be said to be a *relative* moral value, the illusion of "socialist idealism" can be said to be an imaginary moral value; and here "imaginary" is synonymous with "negative." This is perhaps one of the most dramatic aspects of the progress of disenchantment experienced by mankind in the latter half of the twentieth century, as compared to the romantic enthusiasm—not yet entirely dissipated—that flourished in the nineteenth century.

It happens in every age, I believe, that young people

take special delight in shocking their elders. Most of us older people cherish the memory of some incident from our youth by means of which we were able to "express ourselves"—to the horror of our parents. This manifestation of nonconformity took the form of a bizarre vocabulary, of unusual dress, of an unconventional life-style. The pleasure derived from such behavior consisted in not doing what society expected us to; and it was a perfectly normal and ordinary sort of pleasure.

What is happening today, however, goes far beyond that kind of reaction. It is infinitely more widespread and radical. The nonconformity of youth today is not simply a desire to shock. It is not superficial and reactionary. It is a fundamental questioning of man and of life in human society. It is most important that we see this situation in that light and that we do not reject the evidence because it is disturbing. In France during May and June 1968, for example, it was obvious that our young people were not merely trying to shock their elders, or to amuse themselves. The crowds in the streets were not simply students playing at being nonconformists. They were young people of all backgrounds and beliefs, spontaneously and firmly united in rebellion against what is called bourgeois society.

Since "bourgeois society" is the label attached to a certain reality, it should be pointed out that, as a term, it is confusing, and therefore dangerous. Let me explain. Until the middle of the present century, *respectability* was regarded as a prime moral value. This was true not only at a certain (affluent) level of society, but at all levels. It was an almost universal attitude, so much so that the respectability of an individual was regarded as a moral value; that is, a man was respectable if he occupied his proper place within society, in conformity to an ideal of man that was universally recognized as satisfactory. A young man, when he had developed emotionally and had finished his education, "took his place in society," was accepted by others, and, within that context, was allowed to develop. That, essentially, is the concept of respectability. A man was respectable, in the opinion of society, because he knew and observed the rules of the game.

Now the validity of the whole game is being questioned by young people—the whole infinitely complex structure. It is absolutely indispensable that we recognize the truth of this. The rebellion against respectability, however unanimous and universal it may be, is but an expression of that questioning of the entire system.

Let us go one step further. Another value of the old system is the concept of "honor," a concept that was expressed in many different ways, according to a diversity of codes, at a variety of social levels. Honor was perceived as a dominant moral value, and even as *the* dominant one. And yet nothing was more ambiguous than that concept. Often, it meant nothing more than conformity to a certain human ideal; that is, it implied a more or less passive acquiescence in something that had already been decided. And that acquiescence was often regarded as being synonymous with moral goodness. This was, in effect, a very dangerous situation, for, far from forming a good moral conscience, the concept of honor led to a seriously misformed conscience. To observe the rules and regulations of a social group in order to preserve one's "honor" is hardly a contribution to solving man's basic moral problem. And, to make matters worse, this concern with "honor" was identical at both the middle and upper levels of society—a phenomenon that, social implications aside, gives one pause.

In our time, it is indispensable that all of us, whatever our age, become aware of a truth the perception of which characterizes our world. And that truth is this, that, in the light of the human sciences, of events, of an extremely complex civilization, it is clear that if we are to resolve the problem of human insecurity which is the basis of all morality, we must accept as absolute moral values none of the following: possession, power, comfort, consumption, progress, utopian dreams, respectability, and "honor."

4. THE ULTIMATE VALUE: LOVE

Having recited and rejected the litany of "bourgeois" values, what are we left with? Where shall we look now for our true and ultimate moral values? Up into modern times, man tried to establish the nature of that value by a double inquiry. On the one hand, he submitted the question to a philosophical investigation based upon what could be observed more or less empirically, and thus tried to make sense out of the meaning of the universe and of human acts. On the other hand—and this was mixed in with philosophical investigation—he put the question to the Supposedly Knowing Subject—that is, to the deity—or to ancestral tradition.

Today something has caused a radical change, and that is the appearance and development of the human sciences since the beginning of the twentieth century. These sciences have applied to man himself, in all his complex reality, the change in attitude that occurred in the seventeenth century. When modern man wishes to understand, analyze, and grasp the meaning of things, he no longer has recourse to the Supposedly Knowing Subject or to ancestral tradition; instead, he undertakes a scientific, experimental and methodical study of those things. It is interesting to note that this new attitude, by a logical process of evolution, has led man to the study of himself by means of the human sciences. Chief among these sciences, for our purposes, are biology and psychology. That is not to say that the others—sociology, economics, political science, etc.—are unimportant, but that biology and psychology are at the center and source of the most important questions on the dynamics of human behavior.

By biology I mean that aspect of the study of man that considers man in his organic and physiological reality, both structurally and from the viewpoint of evolution. In other words, from the viewpoint of physiological organization, man is an outgrowth of the evolution of the animate world—an outgrowth the modalities and time of which it is extremely difficult, if not impossible, to situate. In any event, this new living being is characterized by a particularly complex central nervous system; so much so that we can say that man's cerebral development is "excessive" in relation to his need for purely physiological adjustment. Man's neuronic relays exist in such superabundance that, at the human level, it seems that there must exist something greater than merely organic life. In the world of man, there are things that cannot be foreseen, that do not correspond directly and exclusively to physiological needs. With respect to the way man lives, he is thus in a position radically different from that of the other animals; and this position, or modality of existence, may be defined as a reflective and investigative knowledge, on man's part, of both his environment and himself. In this context—and not in the old philosophical meaning of the word—we can truly speak of *consciousness.* (One school of Soviet anatomo-physiologists even claims that it can demonstrate the exist-ence of *liberty* by using anatomophysiological data as their premises.)

This reflective and investigative consciousness of man is obviously subjective; every man lives it according to his own experience. It is at this level of individual experience that are situated the data of psychoanalysis which show— and this is the essence of the psychoanalytic contribution —that each of us has his own individual world of emotional experience. It begins at birth (or perhaps even before birth), in profound obscurity, and becomes progressively clearer. And these experiences are derived from the relationship in which the individual exists and to which he must adjust, with the human beings that surround him, and, especially early in life, with his parents.

In order to give an example of the fundamental view-point of modern psychology, we may point out that the child, from the earliest moments of its life—though without having the remotest conscious idea of what it is doing—be-haves spontaneously in such a way as not to lose the love of its mother. This, of course, is only one facet among many, albeit an essential one. It is thus by way of infinitely com-plex and conflictual experience, always relatively resolved, and always leading to the discovery of new conflicts, that the individual's consciousness is established within the framework of lived relationships. The basic relational as-pect of the individual consciousness, and thus of the person, appears more clearly than ever before in human history under the light of modern psychology. The entire process of emotional development, all education (at least in theory), all personal reflection and acceptance of responsibility for one's own acts—everything tends toward the establishment of the broadest and most successful intersubjective relationships possible for the individual. This is to say that each of us, at first *in confuso,* then more or less consciously, and then deliberately (with many mistakes, however), tends to find our fulfillment and our happiness in our relationships with others. These other persons are themselves existing as autonomous subjects, and themselves finding their fulfillment in the same relationships.

The above, obviously, is only a very rapid glance at the complex data of modern psychology, but I am satisfied that I have stated the essence of those data. Freud himself said it even more briefly: it is the function of an analyst to allow his client, who is unhappy with his life, to develop the ability *to love* and *to work.*

The information provided by pathology is always extremely positive, because, by focusing on inadequacies, it shows what *should* be. The dictum of Freud mentioned above, for instance, expresses very well the fact that people are unhappy—or neurotic—precisely because they have not succeeded in integrating themselves into a sufficiently satisfying relational network. To love, in effect, means to participate in a relationship in which two persons, whoever they may be, experience a heightened sense of being. To work is to find a sufficiently satisfying place for oneself in a common effort and in a complex situation—which, basically, is a form of love. Professor Hesnard, in *Psych-analyse du lien interhumain,* points out that the whole concrete human condition, as explored by psychology, tends toward a certain *unity.* Not toward confusion, or toward a confused union, but toward that ideal situation in which each of us and all of us will find ourselves together in such a way that the more we are united the more we are ourselves. It would be easy to show to what degree the human quest, over thousands of years, has been based on exactly that concept. One example, of course, is the effort among nations—however clumsy, contradictory, and per-petually doomed to frustration it may be—to arrive at a means of peaceful coexistence.

From these scattered reflections, we may draw the fol-lowing conclusion, a conclusion that seems beyond dis-pute: from the standpoint of modern anthropology, the basic moral value, and the ultimate motive in human be-havior, is the search for and the development of *love* in the broadest sense of that word.

All the data of modern research transform drastically the concept of what is called "natural morality." In the past, the notion of natural law connoted, at least implicitly, a sort of badly defined entity designated as "nature." The whole point of morality, it seemed, was to act "in con-formity with nature," and to avoid behavior that was "against nature." This concept of morality has persisted to the extent that it is found in *Humanae vitae.* But, if we stop to think about it, this idea of nature is very like that of a divinity whose secrets we cannot penetrate and whose knowledge and power we must respect without under-standing. Paradoxically, this attitude has more than a trace of idolatry in it; it is an evocation of "Mother Nature"—a demigod, or intermediary deity, between God and man. The fact is that what was often taken for "nature" was nothing more than the end result of a very long and complex cultural tradition. And it is here that science is able to dissipate our illusions. This demythologizing process is particularly striking, of course, in the area of sexual morality. What is *natural* for man is what we have been talking about: that basic search for successful social and interpersonal relationships—a search the initiative for which lies with man. To reduce it to what is perhaps too brief a formula: human nature is civilization.

Once this is understood, it becomes clear that there is still a place for "natural morality." We could even say that natural morality now comes into its own. Now, however, "natural" is distinguished from "revealed." There no longer exists anything but man himself, in his uncertainty, searching for answers; for biblical revelation has nothing to do with the concept of a "nature divinity." If we look closely, we see that it is not morality that is revealed, but the omnipotence of creative and saving love.

Christianity, in collaboration with the advances of modern science, and particularly of the human sciences, must now lead us to the point where we can divest ourselves of the last remnants of our instinctive and primitive reliance upon a Supposedly Knowing Subject whose will we are required, in one way or another, to decipher.

5.   SEXUAL PERSPECTIVES

It is almost a cliché to say that the most profound change in attitude wrought by the human sciences, and especially by psychoanalysis, has been in the area of human sexual life. Freud demonstrated that sexuality, in its widest sense, is at the core of human emotional development and of intersubjective relationships at various levels. And, finally, it is at the very heart of the human quest. In a sense, Freud overturned the taboos and demystified sexuality, not by banishing mystery from sexual reality but by destroying the myths of human sexual life.

The reaction to Freud's revolution in "respectable" circles was, as we all know, one of scandalized horror. (And this reaction persists today, in certain areas.) The conflict between the new ideas and these respectable folk was long and brutal; and, in the light of that battle, we can see to what extent man's sexual life has been conditioned in the past, implicitly and sometimes explicitly, by a dualist concept of human reality, a concept whose roots have absolutely nothing in common with biblical revela-

tion. It would be interesting to study how Western thought
was contaminated by this bizarre philosophical concept,
but this is not the place for such a study. For our purposes,
we can assume that that contamination is a fact of history.
Let us say merely that the dualist concept of man implies
that man was created by two gods, one good and the other
evil. The good god created man's soul or mind; the bad god
created his material being, and especially his sexual organs.
Thus, sexuality was something to be feared, something dangerous, if not actually evil in itself. This conviction, as it
appeared in its rather late moralistic formulation (the
earliest of which goes back only to the sixteenth century)
laid down certain precepts that were regarded as beyond
dispute, or that were at least never disputed. It is these
precepts or affirmations that psychoanalysis calls into
question. Let me give one example: the affirmation that
everything in the sexual domain constitutes "grave matter."
This means that every sexual activity that is not in keeping
with the rules established by authority is automatically a
"mortal sin." (Although nobody bothered to explain what
all this signified.) Obviously, with the discoveries of modern
psychology and biology, one no longer thinks of sexual
activity in such terms. Still, some moralists followed that
dualist concept to its logical extreme and affirmed (and
this was not so long ago) that even sexual relations within
marriage were "permitted sins" for the purpose of making
babies. Certainly, such an extreme position did not find
favor with all moral theologians; far from it. Even so, the
pejorative concept of sexuality which that position expresses
so clearly was reflected in traditional sexual morality as a
whole. It is this view of sex as an a priori evil that psy-

choanalysis has dissipated. It is now necessary, therefore, for the whole structure of sexual morality to be rethought along lines totally free of pagan dualism.

In the light of modern scientific data, human sexuality appears as being at once an extension and an expression of the sexual reality of the animate world; but it is also, at the same time, something else very different, something that belongs at the level of the properly human, something that is psychological and spiritual. The first aspect of this that comes to our attention is that human sexual activity of any kind is always essentially relational. Sexual dialogue is a special exchange, with a special intensity and content; but it is nonetheless a dialogue not unlike other dialogues. And by dialogue we mean a confrontation of two individual conscious beings at an infinite variety of levels—levels that may even, eventually, be contradictory.

It is possible for human sexual activity to be experienced by an individual as the inability to enter into real dialogue with another human being, or as an instinctive rejection, based upon a vague sort of fear of confrontation. This attitude results in solitary sexual activity, or masturbation. It is also very likely the attitude that motivates homosexuality, which then becomes the basic inability to enter into a dialogue with a person who is truly an *other* person. For human sexual activity always exists in relation to, or more accurately, as a *relationship* with, another. This relationship may be purely imaginary, as that of the adolescent who indulges in masturbation. Or it can be totally negative, in the sense that the *true* other is eliminated; and this seems to be the basic meaning of the problem of homo-

sexuality. Sexual activity can also be experienced in relation to another subject; and the latter then becomes
spontaneously an object of excitement, an emotional or
sensual provocation, a *thing* in the true sense of the word.
Obviously, in such a case, there is no really relational activity; that is, there is no activity that implies any relation of
love.

On the other hand, when two mutually complemen-
tary beings meet fully (in a relative sense), their sexual
activity is the exact expression of their confrontation and
their reciprocal relationship. When the two subjects live
fully their commitment to one another—i.e., in the relationship of a *couple*—then it is evident that their relationship
is at once selective, exclusive, and definitive. Moreover, it
is lived spontaneously as selective, exclusive, and definitive, at least as far as the couple's intentions are concerned.
We can then say, without fear of exaggeration, that, from
the standpoint of a progressive humanization, the couple,
being one and indissoluble, is engaged in an almost
ideally successful relationship. Thus, it is the relationship
of sexual activity to love, properly speaking, that gives us
the basis for a moral judgment concerning that activity.

At the level of human society, as elsewhere in the animate world, it is clear that sexual activity represents the
power and the ability to create life. It is also clear, however,
that that power and ability, as far as human beings are
concerned, take on the characteristics of a consciousness
or awareness—and, more precisely, an awareness of *duration*. By this I mean that genital fecundity, like all of
life, becomes a *project*. For a couple, the regulation of

genital fecundity—i.e., the reasonable control of the number and intervals of births—assumes a place of primary importance. The couple will live its sexual life, and express its sexual life, in relation to that aspect of their common conduct. Therefore, the couple will build their common life around an intelligently planned fecundity, and that plan will affect all of their mutual sexual contacts.

What seems especially desirable from a moral standpoint, as I see it, is that, in the life of a couple, there be a common effort to reach an agreement regarding the couple's common activities. Against that background, it becomes clear that voluntary contraception, regardless of the technique employed, can be an expression of love, and can promote the unity of a couple. In this sense, contraception can be a developmental experience in the overall emotional atmosphere of family life. What guides the moral conduct of a couple, in this case, is the common and continual effort they make to progress together, by means of dialogue, confrontation, conflicts, and resolutions, in their daily lives. In this way, the couple have a means of judging the value and the orientation of their behavior.

Reflection on anthropological data, and especially on the data of psychoanalysis, demonstrates methodically the existence of two essential aspects of sexuality that lead us toward the perception of a true *mystery:* that is, toward the recognition of a reality that transcends our ability to understand it completely, or to explain it. First of all, sexuality, although it serves to preserve and reproduce individual life, and therefore the existence of the species, is, at the same time, evidence of the essential bio-

logical mortality of the individual. Sexuality expresses
life, and propagates life; but it also reveals, from the appearance of the first protozoa, the basic corruptibility of the
individual living being. It is both the creator of life and
the harbinger of death. Man's realization of this basic ambiguity of sexuality conditions the way in which he lives
his sexual life; and it conditions it far beyond his conscious awareness of it.

The second aspect is related to the first. It is that man
seeks, in sex, the answer to his questions concerning his own
beginnings. When a child asks for information about sex,
what he is doing, in fact, is asking (though perhaps not
consciously), Where did I come from? It is at the sexual
level in its broadest sense—that is, abstracting from genital
expression—that a human being finds himself truly face to
face with the mystery of his origin and his destiny.

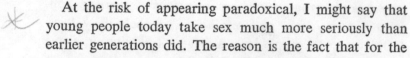

At the risk of appearing paradoxical, I might say that
young people today take sex much more seriously than
earlier generations did. The reason is the fact that for the
past twenty years, the dissemination of psychoanalytic
data has allowed sexual questions to be asked and answered clearly, objectively, and methodically.

It is within the context of this profound change that we
may situate the transformation of moral perspectives. Obviously, young people do not question their sexual conduct
today in the same terms that young people did thirty or
forty years ago. As far as we can tell, and appearances to
the contrary, this change represents progress. Every questioning of moral conduct—a questioning that is natural
to the human condition—involves a choice; i.e., the rejection

of certain ways of behaving and the acceptance of others. The important thing is to discover the basis on which that choice may be made. But, whatever the case, choice implies the rejection, and therefore the prohibition, of certain lines of conduct. It is essential, as far as one's personal moral life is concerned, that this choice, this prohibition, actually be the result of a judgment on the part of the person concerned. In other words, it is necessary that the prohibition of certain acts be based upon a consciousness that is as informed as possible.

Given the advances in sexual enlightenment that have resulted from modern psychology, it is not surprising that young people can no longer accept a negative morality, a morality based solely upon prohibition. What we call "sexual permissiveness" or sexual freedom among young people is simply a reaction against prohibitions imposed from without and based upon a priori judgments that they do not understand. In fact, it is really a matter of *freedom;* in other words, a positive and informed acceptance of responsibility by the individual for his own acts. It would be better, perhaps, to say *autonomy* rather than freedom in sexual matters, for too often sexual freedom among young people is interpreted by older people as nothing more than meaningless license. The fact of the matter is that when young people demand sexual freedom, it is not a question of license but of a search for personal liberty and autonomy in the pursuit of values that are deeply and actually felt.

Anyone who has ever had the opportunity to discuss and exchange ideas with young men and women between the ages of eighteen and twenty-five has been im-

mediately struck by their overriding preoccupation with
the recognition and development of the true values of love.
There are exceptions, to be sure; but almost always one
senses a deep-rooted desire to look beyond the rules and
prohibitions and find the true meaning of sexuality within
a positive context of love. This desire, of course, wreaks
havoc with the pejorative dualism that I referred to a few
pages ago, and therefore with that attitude according to
which sex is a priori evil, or at least suspect.

It might be appropriate, if somewhat shocking, to quote
here a line from *Hair*. The line, which has been widely
quoted, is as follows: "Yes to sex without sin; no to sex
without love." In one sense, the sentiment expressed is
wholly traditional, from a Christian standpoint, whether
one is talking about the content of the Gospels or about
theological speculation such as occurs in the work of
Aquinas. In terms of traditional Christianity, no virtue
has any meaning unless it is, in one way or another, an
expression of love—that is, of charity—at the operative level.
Charity is the form of all virtues. Therefore, what gives its
basic meaning and its positive moral value to sexual activity is that activity's relation to, and its advancement of,
love between two beings. "No to sex without love" is the
exact translation into a modern idiom of an ancient Christian principle. But the other part of the line from *Hair*, "Yes
to sex without sin," conveys the same principle, and is in
complete conformity to scriptural tradition, in asserting
that sex as such is not evil. It is sufficient here to recall the
Genesis recital of creation; sexual reality having been
created, God said that it was good—and even *very good*.

Liberated from taboos and outdated agonies of guilt,

authentic moral deliberation on the meaning of sexuality can now take place in relative freedom. This, in my opinion, is the meaning of the searching that we see among young people today. I think we can safely say that these young people are more keenly aware than their elders of the relationship that can exist between love and a couple's lifelong commitment to one another. Certainly this new moral quest, which seeks to distinguish positive reality (as conflictual and relative as it may be), greatly upsets traditional attitudes. In this regard, however, it is useful to recall that these traditional attitudes, or habits of thought, were themselves greatly influenced by the taboos that we mentioned earlier. It is easy enough to find examples of this change in attitude. One such could well be the present view of masturbation among adolescents, which is no longer regarded as a diabolical manifestation, as some taught that it was, but as a normal exercise in autoeroticism for that stage in life. It is a phase marking the discovery of a new aspect of life; a stage which, at the psychological and erotic level, characterizes personality development. Only twenty years ago, however, a confessor could tell a youth of seventeen who had accused himself of masturbation, "Oh, my poor child! You have crucified Christ!" Today, such an observation would appear ridiculous; for today, an adolescent regards masturbation as a purely personal moral problem.

Light is also being shed in another, more complicated and more significant, area. This is the area of sexual relations before a couple enter into their life together—a problem that admits of extreme variety. This question is often raised by young people, and it is not so easy to give an

answer as it may seem at first glance. Obviously, I have to
treat the subject in an excessively cursory fashion here.
The reality of life, however, is difficult to fit into neat little
categories. Nonetheless, we can distinguish three different
aspects in this sort of sexual activity among young people.
In the first stage, it may be experienced as purely masturbatory—that is, a boy makes use of a partner, any partner,
as a convenience for relieving erotic tension, without recog-
nizing in any way his partner as a person. The obvious
example of this attitude, of course, is that of the young man
who has recourse to a prostitute, the prostitute being, by
definition, a woman-object. It does not take long to conclude that this kind of sexual activity is hardly relational
on the boy's part in the human sense of that term, and this
gives us an idea of the moral value of such activity.

In a second situation, a boy attempts to discover, through
acts that are at once erotic and sentimental (and hesitant),
the mysterious reality of the *other*—that is, of woman. It
is possible that, in this attempt at discovery, the complete
sexual act is both sought and accomplished. It is obvious,
however, that given the context of search and discovery,
this form of sexual activity signifies something different
from that of the boy in the first instance. Instead of being a
rejection of his partner as a person, it is an attempt, however clumsy, to *find* the other as a person. But by its nature,
this attempt is badly conceived and unsuccessful. Moreover,
it carries with it certain risks—particularly the harm that it
may do to the girl, who is herself searching for the meaning
of sexual activity. Even so, this behavior is quite distinct, so
far as moral significance is concerned, from masturbatory
sexual activity; that is, it is aimed at the establishment of

an intersubjective relationship, and thus is not entirely negative. It is not possible, therefore, to answer the question of premarital sexual relations in any absolute or simplistic terms, since different forms of premarital sexual activity have different moral values. When young people ask, "Should one have, or not have, sexual relations before forming a permanent union?" they are not really challenging a prohibition; they are trying to arrive at a deeper understanding of why the prohibition exists.

There is a third possible situation, a situation that is more common, no doubt, in intellectual and student circles than among other, less privileged, groups. Let us say that two young people, in their early twenties, have met, come to know one another, and decided to enter into a mutual commitment as a couple. From a psychological standpoint, they already consider themselves, spontaneously and deliberately, to *be* a couple. However, the fact that they have years of study still ahead of them and that neither of them has any money prevents them from publicly and officially contracting a marriage. Nonetheless, they have sexual relations, and regard those relations as expressing their mutual commitment. It is obvious that their sexual activity has a meaning different from that described in the two previous situations. They are not engaging in what is virtually mutual masturbation; and they are no longer taking part in an agonizing and maladroit search for an *other*. Instead, we may say that their sexual relations actually express the reality of their life together. But there is still missing a certain dimension to their relationship.

Let me give an example in order to clarify what I mean. A young student couple I know of, although not living together, were meeting frequently in order to have sexual relations. At first, they had no scruples about their conduct. But after a certain amount of time, without asking anyone's advice and solely upon their own initiative, they decided to stop having sexual relations. The reason they gave was that they could spend only a certain amount of time together, and that sex left them too little time to talk to one another. Their sexual dialogue had become so intense and all-pervasive that it had kept them from communicating with one another at other levels. To my mind, this example signifies that the couple had realized, at a certain point in their relationship, that the sexual expression of their love could be meaningful only if they could also express themselves and develop freely in other areas as well.

All these changes in attitude, regarding the understanding of sexuality and its significance within a context of interpersonal relationships, require that we rethink, in depth, the traditional data of what used to be called "sexual morality." Certainly, there is much to be clarified and explained; so much, in fact, that we can hardly hope even to begin in these few pages. Nevertheless, it seems to me that it is necessary at least to show to what degree the concept of marriage must be revised at the levels of both human reflection and sacramental significance. If young people protest vehemently against the traditional concept of marriage, we must not think that such protests are purely negative. What often happens is that young people regard the traditional, official, institutional marriage bond as an obligation imposed from without by social structures; and they are not very sure of the place in their present lives, or in their future, of these structures.

The psychological significance of marriage, however, is something quite different, and it presents marriage in a new light. From this standpoint, when a man and a woman, both adults, ask the human society in which they live to recognize the reality of their mutual commitment, they are attaining the highest possible stage in their respective and common emotional and sexual development. In other words, when a young man is married in the presence of a competent representative of society, the act of marriage signifies that the adult world must now recognize the existence of the youth's sexual personality at the same level as that of his father. If we wanted to express it in the jargon of psychoanalysis, we could say that marriage is the final phase in the resolution of a castration complex.

It should be obvious that a great change is necessary in the traditional, social, cultural, and liturgical concept of marriage as defined by Christian tradition. It is not a question of doubting the ultimate moral value of marriage as defined by Christian tradition. On the contrary, the Christian ideal of a man and woman realizing to the maximum degree an interpersonal relationship characterized by exclusiveness and fidelity seems extremely desirable. What we must learn to do, however, is allow young people to perceive that ideal by allowing them the freedom—that is, the interior autonomy—to discover it for themselves.[1]

[1] It is appropriate to end these reflections by remarking that prudery and legalism in sexual matters greatly hinder knowledge and understanding of such matters. Prudery, in the most negative sense of the term, characterizes Marxism today in very much the same way that it characterized Catholic moral theology in the last century. In fact, in both instances, prudery had the same source; for when one loses contact with the person and teaching of Christ as expressed in biblical revelation, one becomes afraid of sex; and, at that point, one's moral attitude must necessarily be negative.

6. A DRAMATIC MORALITY

We have implied repeatedly in the preceding chapters that a workable system of morality must be based upon man's search for successful interpersonal relationships. We have also noted that this morality, in whatever domain it may be sought, essentially does not admit of perfect realization. This is the core of the human quest—and, no doubt, the most dramatic, if not the most tragic, aspect of it. Man's realization of his inability to attain his ideals is certainly not a recent discovery. What modern science has contributed, however, is that this basic contradiction in the human condition is more noticeable today than ever before—thanks largely to the rigorous honesty of scientific observation. It seems to me that this awareness, this perception, of our inability to achieve what our essence requires that we achieve is the root cause of human anguish, even more than the riddle of death or the enigma of suffering. It leads to a question that may at first glance seem foolish: "What good is morality, and why should we try to be moral beings, when any moral effort on our part is doomed to failure?"

If we admit, in effect, that the ideal of happiness exists within the context of perfect interpersonal relations, then we are indeed forced to conclude that it is all an exercise in futility; that is, that we will never find happiness, and, even worse, that we are incapable of being happy. The fact is that, for each of us, relationships unfold in many different ways and at a great variety of levels, and that relational contradictions exist in practice more often than we are aware of it. We very frequently find ourselves in situations where relational ties are mutually exclusive, or at least mutually and profoundly uncomfortable. It is important for us to understand this aspect of human existence, for, underlying youth's more or less explosive restlessness, one will no doubt find a confused (but sometimes very explicit) recognition of this contradictory aspect of human nature—an aspect that, in its extreme form, is readily conducive to despair.

As I have said, we often find ourselves in contradictory situations. An example: I am sitting in my office, listening attentively to a visitor who had an appointment. The ideal accomplishment of our relationship lies in the success of our dialogue, or in our being together and, at the same time, asserting our individuality, our own personalities and abilities. In other words, our encounter is helping both of us to grow as human beings. Then, suddenly, the telephone rings. The caller takes several minutes of my time and of my attention, without knowing that someone else is in my office. My relationship to the caller, like that to the visitor, develops in an atmosphere of mutual awareness.

This means that I must devote myself to establishing the same kind of relationship with the caller as I have with the visitor. Then, while I am still on the telephone, the doorbell rings. (This is a situation familiar to every doctor, lawyer, psychologist, priest, etc.) I asked the caller to excuse me and I answer the door. A client is there, asking for an immediate appointment. In other words, he is asking me for a relationship based on interpersonal exchange; a request that I can grant only by forgetting about my first visitor and my telephone caller. It is obvious at this point that I have become involved in three relationships that are essentially and literally incompatible. I will either have to throw out my first visitor and concentrate on the second one, or forget about both of them and talk to the man on the telephone, or tell two of them that I cannot talk to them at that moment. What this means is that, if I am to engage in a profitable interpersonal relationship with one of those persons, I will have to refuse to become involved in two new relationships that are, a priori, as important and as valid as the first one. All I can hope for is to be able to explain the situation to the telephone caller and the second visitor in such a way as to avoid offending them, or at least to cause as little offense as possible. The damage that I do to the two last persons may be held to a minimum if I am tactful about it; but there is damage, nonetheless. So far as my own equilibrium is concerned, I must learn not to feel guilty, even subconsciously, about being compelled, in such circumstances, to turn people away. (And this is only a tiny facet of the complexities of affective relationships.)

This situation is typical of what happens in everyday life. I am frequently in situations of conflict, situations that I am unable to resolve in a way that everyone involved will find completely satisfactory. Ideally, I should be able to place myself entirely and simultaneously at the disposal of each of my three clients—but, practically, that is *impossible*. And this incapacity is not peculiar to me. No one can acquiesce in three separate and simultaneous demands for love (in the broad sense of that term).

The same basic situation obtains on the more complex level of group relations or international relations. In all these relationships, there is a fundamental and all-pervasive element of ambivalence; there is always *something* that cannot be parceled out without being diminished—something, in other words, that is *limited*, and that therefore has to do with *time*. And this is one of the most disconcerting aspects of our world. We are trying every means of attaining unity, of establishing peace among men and nations, of avoiding terrible confrontations like those of the past half century; and yet, at the same time, in the midst of our efforts, we understand one another so little that wars (at least "local wars") continue to break out and be fought with the same frequency and intensity as ever. As Hesnard remarks, mankind is obsessed with the idea of achieving unity through understanding, and, at the same time, mankind finds that it is incapable of attaining that unity. The somewhat naïve and imaginative hippie movement is actually an aggravated symptom of dissatisfaction, if not of deep anguish, in the face of man's inability fully to realize his ideal.

Given this situation—a situation which requires an increasingly rigorous intellectual honesty—it seems to me very important that we find the courage to admit the existence of this interior contradiction and to see it as it is. When we are talking about morals, especially—that is, when we are discussing the meaning of human acts with young people—it is absolutely essential that we recognize the situation for what it is. We can no longer imprison youth within the a priori categories of a legalistic morality that has worked only for past generations. But we must recognize also that we cannot, under the pretext of being "with it," lead them toward a sort of romantic idealism the results of which would undoubtedly be catastrophic.

If we are to arrive at a relatively clear view of the basic lack of understanding among men (as manifested in both individual and group relations), we must rely upon the scientific knowledge resulting from Freud's discoveries. These discoveries shed light, a cruel light, on this situation, by giving us a better understanding of *how* man is unsuccessful in understanding man, even though they do not tell us *why* he is unsuccessful.

If one is to be fully himself with another person, and if he is to allow that other person also to be fully himself, it is obviously necessary for the distance between the two subjects to be known; that is, we must locate, clearly and precisely, the limit or frontier at which one person may exist without confusing himself, subconsciously, with another. This, however, is precisely what is impossible, because of the way in which an individual's emotional life develops in relation to another individual. (And the discovery of this development is the essential contribution of psychoanalysis.) It is not possible for us to discuss this basic question at length in these few pages; but we can sum the

ambivalence of human emotional development by saying
that, from the beginning, from birth and the first few
months of its life, an infant can exist as a conscious being
only by confusing itself, partially, with another being.
The latter, at least initially, is usually the mother; and the
infant at first (and of necessity) is unaware of where the
"I" ends and the "other" begins.

Within a short time—a shorter time, no doubt, than adult
observation admits—the infant becomes aware of the
mystery of *language;* that is, of the more or less structured
means through which one individual consciousness is able
to communicate with another individual consciousness in
a reciprocal and self-renewing exchange. If we admit this
very broad definition of language, then we see immediately
that language, too, is very ambivalent. Language permits
one consciousness to communicate to another (individually
or collectively) something of itself; that is, language allows
us to reveal an aspect of ourselves to another. But, *at the
same time,* this reciprocal revelation makes both individuals aware that there is much more that cannot be revealed.
In other words, the power to communicate with another
human being exposes our basic inability to communicate
truly and fully. And this ambivalence of human language
is built into language; it is an essential part of it. If, therefore, we are ever to attain total, perfect reciprocal communication, it will have to be by going beyond a language
that is inexact, partial, and confusing. Actually, we sometimes experience this phenomenon of going beyond language in our everyday lives. We have all experienced and
participated in emotions—an overwhelming sense of joy, let

us say—where we recognized that the best way to react was to be silent; that is, to go beyond the limits imposed by explicit discourse.

This basic and inescapable ambivalence, however, is itself nothing more than a single aspect of an ambivalence that is even deeper and more radical; an ambivalence that Freud clarified by his successive descriptions of the principle of pleasure and of reality, and to which he applied the somewhat debatable name of "death wish." It seems to me that there is something intuitional, a literally scientific perception, something absolutely fundamental, in Freud's approach. If we transpose his terms a bit, we see that he is working not within a philosophical context, but within that of direct knowledge, of the essential dialectic of subjective consciousness of *duration*. From the first clumsy reactions of a child to the most spontaneous reactions of an adult, everything happens as though man, both individually and collectively, tends to operate within the never ending dialectic of concrete duration, and, at the same time, to dominate that dialectic, to "deny" it, so to speak, by virtue of a longing for stability which is never satisfied. We are conscious beings who require a progressive development of our selves; and, at the same time, we feel a deep need for "eternity"—that is, for a perennial status quo, free from the agonizing limitations of time and existential duration. The explicit awareness of the ego is at once the consciousness and the negation of the human necessity for gradual development which must end, eventually, in death.

In my opinion, it is absolutely indispensable for us today

to emphasize that every discussion or reflection on morality takes place in the shadow of that double ambivalence. It is necessarily so; and there is nothing that we can do about it.

It is striking to what extent the observations and comments in the preceding paragraphs evoke the specter of the ancient concept known as the doctrine of original sin, and perhaps shed new light on it. The human condition, as an observable phenomenon, is self-contradictory in its own dynamics; it is situated in time, and yet claims to conquer and dominate time. The religious formulation of that basic concept has been expressed, up to modern times, by a special system of images and vocabulary. The idea of man's "fall" from a supposedly superior state had been a dominant one until the modern age. However, we can no longer see things as simply as that. We now know that there was no "golden age" of man, no "earthly paradise," no "superior state" from which man fell by "sin." The truth is infinitely more complex than that. It is also infinitely more unexplainable. We find hints of this fact in the writings of a man who lived long before modern times, but who, it seems, experienced the human contradiction with particular intensity. In very "modern" language, St. Paul recorded several thoughts that seem out of keeping with the spirit of his age:

> I cannot understand my own behavior. I fail to carry out the things I want to do, and I myself doing the very things I hate. When I act against my own will, that means I have a self that acknowledges that the Law is good, and so the thing behaving

in that way is not my self but sin living in me. The fact is, I know of nothing good living in me—living, that is, in my unspiritual self—for though the will to do what is good is in me, the performance is not, with the result that instead of doing the good things I want to do, I carry out the sinful things I do not want. When I act against my will, then it is not my true self doing it, but sin which lives in me.

In fact, this seems to be the rule, that every single time I want to do good it is something evil that comes to hand. In my inmost self I dearly love God's Law, but I can see that my body follows a different law that battles against the law which my reason dictates. This is what makes me a prisoner of that law of sin which lives inside my body.

What a wretched man I am! Who will rescue me from this body doomed to death? [Romans 7:15–24]

It would be superfluous to point out that, in this text, the word "sin," strictly speaking, has no *moralistic* overtones. It is not a question of faults of which Paul may accuse himself of having committed through his own will. He is talking about something completely different: about a mystery of contradiction that is, in Romans, almost personified. "Sin" is presented as a "thing" that acts against man's will: "It is not my true self doing it, but sin which lives in me." And yet it is man who acts. The traditional formulation expresses this fact in its own way; and now we are trying to articulate, in another way, the same fact, that this drama of contradiction has its origin in man himself.

If we intend to talk with young people about morality, it would perhaps be well to ask ourselves a question before-

hand: What is it that we intend to do? Do we want to com-
pel young people to accept a system of mental categories
that we ourselves have found more or less satisfying, and
that will appease our interior insecurity? Or do we want
to turn over to them, in a spirit of brotherly love, the
fruits of our own human experience and of our own open-
ended quest? The message of Christianity, properly speaking, as it emerges from the total dynamic of biblical
revelation, does not consist in a *teaching* of morality. This
message does not lay down the rules of human behavior.
The dynamics of human behavior have always sprung
from a search by man within man, and from man's understanding of his interior tensions. Biblical revelation sheds
light on that search—a light that focuses most dramatically
on a few sentences from the writings of St. Paul. Man did
not wait for the appearance of the Bible to begin searching
for a behavioral norm with all that it implies. Nor did he
wait for Freud to become aware that this search was difficult, and that there was an unexplainable contradiction
within himself. By a diversity of means, man has always
perceived that his destiny was to succeed in loving. And,
by a diversity of means, man has always known that he
would never succeed in loving. And yet, in all cultures,
and through all modalities of expression, the human obses-
sion has always been the same: to try to succeed, in one
way or another, in loving fully. The modern formulation
which Dr. Hesnard expresses so well in his book is nothing
but a more accurate articulation of this fundamental truth
of the human condition. The maximum realization of
interpersonal relationships at every level—this is an ideal

that is expressed quite simply in the biblical and evangelical exhortation, "Love your neighbor as yourself." Biblical revelation, as incarnated in the person of Jesus, contributes the certitude that this love, which is the object of our longing, does, in fact, *exist;* that it existed before anything else; and that it is love that causes *us* to exist.

Biblical revelation, in its most authentic sense, does not attempt to allay human anguish by sending man to a Supposedly Knowing Being who wields the authority of power. It reveals *love* itself, in the historical person of Jesus. This fact transforms radically the uneasy concept of human anguish that we call *guilt.* And here we literally go beyond the concept of human anguish based (from a Freudian viewpoint) upon an image of a father possessing the authority to forbid his son to be, or to exist. In other words, and again within the Freudian context, there is a transformation in the concept of paternity. There is no longer a Supposedly Knowing Subject who punishes man when man does not understand what this Being wants. There is now a love which is much greater than our human potential; a love that penetrates into man's being by every means (including death) in order to help man attain the fullness of love. In the Song of Songs, it is said that love is as strong as death. Death's strength is derived from the fact that it has the final word; it is the end of life. By the same reasoning, love is as strong as death, for it has the really final word—over death as well as life. This is the final, specific, and indeed the *only* meaning of biblical revelation. In my opinion, it is no exaggeration to say that it is thanks to the data of the human sciences, and especially

to modern psychology, that this meaning of biblical
revelation emerges clearly—and emerges from a secular
culture that more or less contained that revelation, but
contaminated it with moralism, rationalism, or legalism.
Thus, the unique and fundamental need for love is perceived by modern man with as much intensity and clarity
as man's inability to love fully is perceived.

This perception, as far as its impact on man's moral
efforts is concerned, will be of great help in transforming
our lives. In our daily lives, if we know that "we are loved
by love" (which is the deepest meaning of faith), we will
no longer live as in the same way as before. A comparison
may be helpful here. A man who is truly loved by his wife
and friends, and who truly loves them, will be very at-
tentive to other people because he is emotionally secure; he
will not live in the same way as a man who is not loved, or
who does not *know* that he is loved. On every occasion,
joyful or otherwise, he will be aware that he is loved. He
will ask his wife or his friends, either explicitly or by his
attitude, for an expression of love; and that expression will
give him the strength to act and the courage to undergo
trials. This is perhaps the true meaning of *prayer*. A man
who knows that he is loved by Love itself, in Christ, will no
longer live as he did before, and he will ask (i.e., *pray*)
Love to help him love more fully. This is the practical
meaning of a disturbing sentence from Paul's letter to the
Romans: "For I am certain of this: neither death nor life,
no angel, no prince, nothing that exists, nothing still to
come, not any power, or height or depth, nor any created
thing, can ever come between us and the love of God made
visible in Christ Jesus our Lord" [8:38–39].

Yet, the fact remains that man's effort to love is, of itself, doomed to disappointment. Another aspect of Christian revelation is concerned with precisely this point; and it is here that the traditional notion of "salvation" belongs. Obviously, we can no longer conceive of salvation in a legalistic sense. Rather, it is a matter of understanding accurately, in the person of Jesus and his history (to the extent that it can be understood in the pertinent documents), the message of love triumphant over death, which is the supreme sign of love. "A man can have no greater love than to lay down his life for his friends" [John 15:13]. This is the heart and the whole of the Christian message. Here, there is a complete transformation of the concepts of fear, uncertainty, anguish and guilt. In fact, according to biblical revelation, it was not "the Father" who crucified Jesus, but men. But it was "the Father" who raised him up from the dead; that is, who demonstrated that his existence was triumphant over death.

I may say once again, without going into any more explanations, that all these observations are suggested by the data of the human sciences of our day. These data lead us to view the concepts of sin, guilt, salvation (i.e., pardon), in a truly and totally new light in comparison with the legalistic and juridical approach of past centuries. It seems to me beyond debate that this new approach is much more in conformity than the old one with the whole of biblical revelation. And, as far as a concept of morality for young people is concerned, it is obvious that we need, at this same level of consideration, a very deep and thorough rethinking of the concept of sin and of what we call "the sacrament of penance." Far from destroying the meaning or the value of such concepts, it seems evident that this new approach will help us to grasp, with a much greater degree of accuracy than ever before, their truly *supernatural* meaning.

CONCLUSION

Amid the anguished uncertainty that pervades the present age, it is of overriding importance, if we are to arrive at a systematic understanding of man as man, to declare, loudly and at length, that love, in its broadest meaning, is the only value capable of dynamizing man's acts and his moral strivings. From the standpoint of "Christian doctrine," we must demonstrate that this concept of love is in direct conformity with divine revelation, and that the specific difference of the Christian message is *hope*. Basically, the specifically Christian aspect of morality is simply the integration, into a supremely important whole, of acts, moral sense, and "time." If we wish to have an authentic and concretely Christian outlook, each of us, individually and collectively, must weld together our uncertainty—which is the source of our acts—and our hope. And hope, properly speaking, is the profound belief that love exists, and conquers all, in the person of Christ Jesus. This belief makes it possible for us to be attentively conscious of the needs of the present, and, at the same time, to be ever aware of the reality that exists beyond time—a reality that is, nonetheless, contained in the present.

POSTFACE
by R. Simon

The dictionary defines a postface as a commentary located at the end of a book. This, however, is a postface only by courtesy. Its purpose is not so much to comment on M. Oraison's thoughts as it is to expand them somewhat and to highlight certain of his themes. In other words, it is intended to be a sort of dialogue with the author, who, as it happens, is also a friend; but a dialogue limited by the exigencies of space.

M. Oraison has been endowed with the gift of devising striking formulas—a gift that is at once a strength and a weakness. Its strength lies in its ability to cut straight to the heart of a question; and its weakness is that it tends to oversimplify. One of these formulas seems particularly interesting; I mean that of the Supposedly Knowing Subject. This concept strikes out against a deformed idea of God and Providence, an idea very similar to that which has been the target of the attacks of Marxists and Freudians. This idea or image of God is more or less identified with a divine omniscience and omnipotence that is regarded as concurrent with human knowledge and power. It is this idea that M. Oraison's formula is intended to denounce—an idea that resulted in an attitude, among churchmen, to the effect that such events as the Galileo affair, the appearance of the natural and human sciences, the advent of democratic government and the disappearance of a certain kind of social hierarchy, the secularization of values (including moral values), were all sacrilegious annexations of domains that had, up until then, been part of the empire of God.

The formula of a Supposedly Knowing Subject is directed also against an attitude that is a corollary to such a concept of God; that is, a refusal to take the initiative, a flight from responsibility, and, consequently, a possible acquiescence in social injustice for the sake, and in the name, of peace, law, order, and tranquillity. No doubt, under this aspect M. Oraison's formula is founded upon recent history; for let us remember that the prophets of the nineteenth century were named Proudhon, Saint-Simon, Karl Marx—and it was their aim to mobilize the working classes that the church had lost.

The formula of a Supposedly Knowing Subject presents another, and somewhat unexpected, aspect, inasmuch as it coincides with an important facet of the traditional concept of "natural law." St. Thomas, speaking of natural law, taught that man, because of his reasoning power and his liberty, has a certain peculiarity of being: he is *providentia sui et sibi* (providence for himself and of himself). This means that, as a reasonable creature, man has the knowledge and the ability to control his acts. It is therefore man's responsibility to use his intellect and his will in order to define his objectives and to determine the means he will use to attain those objectives. At the basis of every moral act, there is a certain well of ethical intuitions that are indispensable to, and make possible, any judgment of value. There exists, in addition to this inalienable basis of judgment, an enormous collection of laws, decisions, and options, both individual and collective, that are the result of painstaking intellectual research and practical experimentation.

It goes without saying (and M. Oraison, in effect, has not said it) that man's intellect and his free will do not eliminate Providence. Providence still has a role to play in the consciousness of believers, just as the concept of obedience to God's will has a role to play. It would be foolish to deny, however, that these two concepts—of Providence and "God's will"—have been greatly abused. The recital of these abuses is too lengthy to undertake here. But, to put it briefly, let us say that obedience to the will of God sends one to two places: to the Word of God as expressed by the church, with all its difficulties, questions, and interpretations; or to the world, with all its values, history, hopes, anguish, and sin. The existence of this double frame of reference emphasizes the difficulty of thinking and living in obedience to faith. What can we say to prove that such faith is not merely an admission of ignorance in the face of the unknown, a subordination of one's intellect to the unknown and, as yet, unmastered forces of nature?

Submission to destiny (whatever term may be used to describe that condition) is easily distinguishable from the obedience that springs from faith. The latter finds its

source in an encounter with that absolute Other whom we
call God. It vanquishes the will to be self-sufficient and
leads, with him, onto the road of life and into an adventure
that surpasses our prudent little plans and expectations.
The path of obedience is, essentially, the path of love. It
led Peter from a fisherman's boat to a martyr's death; and
it led Paul from the persecution of Christians to the preach-
ing of the Gospel and, finally, to a Roman prison. Such obedience is not made, nor is it given; and, for that reason, it
is impossible for such faith to remain within the secure
shelter simply of observing the law. Obviously, it does
not replace the law, for the law is necessary inasmuch as
we are sinners and we must somehow live together; but it
is beyond the law. It is motivated by something more than
a respect for rules and regulations. It has its source in the
presence of the Other, in the hearing of his word, and in
the experience of a faithfulness, a loyalty, that is like no
other.

M. Oraison has been saying all these things for a long
time, in his own way. What he opposes, paradoxically, is
everything that hinders the creative surge of life, that impedes the movement and the dynamics of love. His critique
is aimed at all those who refuse to see things as they are
because they would then be forced to begin an agonizing
revision of their own thinking. His present work continues
in the same vein, as evidenced by his use of the formula of
the Supposedly Knowing Subject.

A related formula is that of Mother Nature, or the
"nature-divinity." Here, M. Oraison's target is the mythological halo that the concept of nature has somehow pre-
served over the centuries, by virtue of which it is regarded as

a sort of intermediary reality between God and man. According to that concept, nature is an open book in which man must learn to read the will of God. Man has become rather skeptical about this, and the phenomenon of secularization and desacralization has made us critical of the naïve "finalism" of the preclassical age. What we would have to do now would be to distinguish at length the various meanings of "nature"; and, obviously, this is not the place to undertake that task. I will say only that, in the expression "natural law," the word "natural" signifies the core of immutable values that cannot be questioned without doing great harm to man in his very being and with respect to his destiny. It is in no way a question of "natural" structures or functions such as are studied by the modern sciences. But it is true that, in determining the content of the "natural law," one must take into account *all* the elements—i.e., biological, physiological, psychological, etc.—that constitute a human being. Even so, it is not possible for a "natural" datum, the end result of a natural function, to be regarded as a moral law. It is against this impossible transition from the natural to the moral that M. Oraison inveighs. His way of looking at things does not do away with an objective ethical rule, but simply situates that objective rule within the complex network of interpersonal and intercommunal relationships that is dominated by the Gospel commandment of love. These relationships are the realities that assure personal development and constitute the objective frame of reference of moral conduct. Biological realities form part of this frame of reference as integrating elements, but they are never, of themselves, a norm of moral behavior. This can be borne out by many examples. One

might wish that the author had examined this question
more fully.

Since the author denounces, and with reason, moral
theologians' abuse of the concepts of "nature" and "natural
law," it comes as no surprise to see that of nature reappear
in his analysis of the laws of human development—laws
the general lines of which he sketches out in psychoanalytic terms. It is true, as the author recognizes without saying it explicitly, that we cannot throw out entirely the
concept of "nature," since the human person is an indissoluble composite of nature and freedom. It is important to
note, however—and this distinction is of some importance
—that M. Oraison's analyses have to do with the meaning of
man and the laws of human development. But a judgment
of value cannot be based purely upon description; happiness, which the author offers as the final end of human acts,
is neither a datum nor the simple result of psychological de-
terminism. It is, within the limitations imposed by the human condition, the object of a conscious choice.

To these remarks I should like to add two shorter ones.
M. Oraison's purpose is to present the problem of human
behavior as a field to be investigated, the development of
man as a history under construction, and morality as a
reflection on the dynamism of that investigation and that
history. In the author's thought, therefore, the laws of
morality have the same flexibility as life itself and human
evolution, and the acts of an individual take their moral
value from the overall orientation of the individual. Which
is to say that the principles of human conduct are energized
from the same source as human conduct itself. From that
standpoint, one is in a position to appreciate at its true

value what the author has to say about the principle of totality. Conjugal life is a life project involving a couple, and fecundity constitutes an essential dimension of that project. It is up to the couple to space out their children so as to ensure the proper development of the family. They must preserve the full value of their relationship and, at the same time, control the birth of their children. It is M. Oraison's opinion that, for this purpose, the use of contraceptives is legitimate. Out of respect for *Humanae vitae,* one might consider this question from the standpoint of spiritual growth. The gap that might open up between the couple's practice and the rule laid down by the encyclical will certainly have to be bridged. This does not mean, however, that one can judge the conduct of two conscious beings who may very well be firmly established on the path of evangelical perfection.

One might very well say approximately the same thing about premarital relations. Here, again one must take into account the intentions and the overall goal of the young man and young woman. M. Oraison is careful to distinguish between cases; and, in fact, one cannot judge the moral value of all premarital relations in the exact same light. It is extremely difficult even to give a brief answer to this problem, for an answer depends upon a whole complex of questions that are being asked today about marriage and the sacrament of marriage. What one can say is that the concept of Christian marriage involves the fidelity of the two partners. We also know that this ideal is difficult to realize, and that it requires, from the very beginning, a measure of asceticism and discipline; for sex, like everything else, must be lived under the sign of the cross and of redemption. It is from this perspective that one must consider the positive value of sexual abstinence once a man and woman have become engaged to be married. M. Oraison does not deny the existence of that value; but it would have been interesting to read his thoughts on its psychological conditions.

These are the thoughts I have had while reading this book. Certainly, there are many other things that deserve to be said, but I have not had sufficient space to say all of them. It therefore remains only for me to wish the reader a maximum profit from the perusal of this work, and to urge him to regard the book as an invitation to personal reaction and criticism. This is, no doubt, the wish also of the author; for I know him well enough to know that he has no pretensions to being a Supposedly Knowing Subject.

R. Simon
Professor, *Institut Catholique*

APPENDIX

ROMANS
THE LETTER OF PAUL
TO THE CHURCH IN ROME
(CHAPTER 7)

THE CHRISTIAN IS NOT BOUND BY THE LAW

1 Brothers, those of you who have studied law will know
2 that laws affect a person only during his lifetime. ·A married woman, for instance, has legal obligations to her husband while he is alive, but all these obligations come to an
3 end if the husband dies. ·So if she gives herself to another man while her husband is still alive, she is legally an adulteress; but after her husband is dead her legal obligations come to an end, and she can marry someone else without
4 becoming an adulteress. ·That is why you, my brothers, who through the body of Christ are now dead to the Law, can now give yourselves to another husband, to him who rose
5 from the dead to make us productive for God. ·Before our conversion our sinful passions, quite unsubdued by the Law,

⁶ fertilized our bodies to make them give birth to death. ·But now we are rid of the Law, freed by death from our imprisonment, free to serve in the new spiritual way and not the old way of a written law.

THE FUNCTION OF THE LAW

⁷   Does it follow that the Law itself is sin? Of course not. What I mean is that I should not have known what sin was except for the Law. I should not for instance have known what it means to covet if the Law had not said *You shall not* ⁸ *covet*. ·But it was this commandment that sin took advantage of to produce all kinds of covetousness in me, for when there is no Law, sin is dead.

⁹   Once, when there was no Law, I was alive; but when the ¹⁰ commandment came, sin came to life ·and I died: the commandment was meant to lead me to life but it turned out to ¹¹ mean death for me, ·because sin took advantage of the commandment to mislead me, and so sin, through that commandment, killed me.

¹²   The Law is sacred, and what it commands is sacred, just ¹³ and good. ·Does that mean that something good killed me? Of course not. But sin, to show itself in its true colors, used that good thing to kill me; and thus sin, thanks to the commandment, was able to exercise all its sinful power.

THE INWARD STRUGGLE

¹⁴   The Law, of course, as we all know, is spiritual; but I am ¹⁵ unspiritual; I have been sold as a slave to sin. ·I cannot understand my own behavior. I fail to carry out the things I want to do, and I find myself doing the very things I hate. ¹⁶ ·When I act against my own will, that means I have a self

[17] that acknowledges that the Law is good, ·and so the thing
[18] behaving in that way is not my self but sin living in me. ·The
fact is, I know of nothing good living in me—living, that is,
in my unspiritual self—for though the will to do what is
[19] good is in me, the performance is not, ·with the result that
instead of doing the good things I want to do, I carry out
[20] the sinful things I do not want. ·When I act against my will,
then, it is not my true self doing it, but sin which lives in me.
[21]   In fact, this seems to be the rule, that every single time
[22] I want to do good it is something evil that comes to hand. ·In
[23] my inmost self I dearly love God's Law, but ·I can see that
my body follows a different law that battles against the law
which my reason dictates. This is what makes me a prisoner
of that law of sin which lives inside my body.
[24]   What a wretched man I am! Who will rescue me from this
[25] body doomed to death? ·Thanks be to God through Jesus
Christ our Lord!
    In short, it is I who with my reason serve the Law of God,
and no less I who serve in my unspiritual self the law of sin.